# EXPLORING the HIDDEN CHARLES

## A Guide to Outdoor Activities on Boston's Celebrated River

## MICHAEL TOUGIAS

APPALACHIAN MOUNTAIN CLUB BOOKS
BOSTON, MASSACHUSETTS

Cover Photograph: Scott Underhill
All photographs by the author unless otherwise noted
Cover Design: Elisabeth Leydon Brady
Book Design: Carol Bast Tyler
© 1997 Michael Tougias. All rights reserved.

Distributed by The Globe Pequot Press, Inc., Old Saybrook, CT

Published by the Appalachian Mountain Club. No part of this publication may be reproduced or transmitted in any form or by any means, electronic or mechanical, including photocopying and recording, or by any information storage or retrieval system, except as may by expressly permitted by the 1976 Copyright Act or in writing from the publisher. Requests for permission should be addressed in writing to Appalachian Mountain Club Books, 5 Joy Street, Boston, MA 02108.

*Library of Congress Cataloging-in-Publication Data*
Tougias, Mike, 1955–
    Exploring the hidden Charles: a guide to outdoor activities on Boston's celebrated river / Michael Tougias.
        p.   cm.
    Includes bibliographical references (p.   ) and index.
    ISBN 1-878239-60-0 (alk. paper)
        1. Outdoor recreation—Massachusetts—Charles River—Guidebooks. 2. Charles River (Mass.)—Guidebooks. I. Title.
GV191.42.M4T68    1997
917.44'4—dc21                                              97-28450
                                                              CIP

The paper used in this publication meets the minimum requirements of the American National Standard for Information Sciences—Permanence of Paper for Printed Library Materials, ANSI Z39.48–1984.∞

**Due to changes in conditions,
use of the information in this book
is at the sole risk of the user.**

Printed on recycled paper using soy-based inks.
Printed in the United States of America.

10  9  8  7  6  5  4  3  2  1              97  98  99  00  01  02

# Contents

# Acknowledgments

F IRST OF ALL, I want to thank my wife, Mary Ellen, who helped in so many ways while I was writing or out having fun on the river. Many friends and family members also offered their support, and more than a few accompanied me on my many trips to the Charles. Jon Cogswell, Stanley Buzarewicz, and my brother Mark all made my river visits more enjoyable.

Research of the Charles could not have been completed without the help of a great many knowledgeable individuals. The material prepared by the Charles River Watershed Association was especially helpful, and the hard-working members of the association have my sincere thanks for protecting the river.

Finally, I wish to thank my friends at AMC Books— Gordon Hardy, Ola Frank, Elisabeth Brady, and Carol Tyler—for making this new edition a wonderful reality.

# Prologue

People have always loved rivers. Thoreau described them as "a constant lure, when they flow by our door, to distant enterprise and adventure." My constant lure has been the Charles, a river rich in history and tradition. But, for me, the Charles is much more than that—it is a vehicle for surprise and adventure, with a diversity unlike that of any other river.

Most people's concept of the Charles has been formed by that portion of the river that flows through Boston. To the west of the city, however, the river is quite different; in some places it runs through areas so secluded it's hard to believe this is the same Charles. Both parts of the river have much to offer—the fact that the lower portion is seen and enjoyed by hundreds of thousands of people while the upper portion is something of a secret gives the Charles a character all its own.

Most of my free time has been spent on the Charles rather than racing from one attraction to another. I guess that makes me a "river rat." I'm drawn to rivers because of their ever changing moods, from tranquil, slow-flowing waters to turbulent, singing rapids. Within the eighty-mile length of the Charles, the river and surrounding terrain undergo a variety of transformations. Canoeing through the Norfolk and Millis stretch of the river in the summer gives

*A great blue heron takes flight.*

*My sturdy Old Town Pack canoe.*

one the feeling of the tropics. The overhanging foliage of maples and oaks crowds the river's main channel, forming a green, junglelike canopy. Farther downstream in Sherborn the hemlock trees and steep cliffs of Rocky Narrows provide a setting more reminiscent of the upland forests of northern New England. And then there's Long Ditch in Dedham, a canal built by colonial settlers connecting the Charles in two different spots. The ditch passes through the heart of Cutler Marsh, where the tall marsh grass growing in the flat flood plain makes you feel like you're on a Kansas prairie.

I've been exploring the Charles for twenty years and I'm still not sure I've uncovered all its secrets. But I do know that I don't have to go to Alaska or some remote island to find adventure and beauty; often they're right outside my door.

I've come to view the Charles as a microcosm of New England: its geography, its history, and its wildlife. One can better understand a region by viewing it from a canoe seat than a car seat—besides, the fishing is a heck of a lot better. Too many of us take only a quick look at the river; I decided to take a long look *from* the river.

# Large Reservations along the Charles

T=Trustees of Reservation     A=Massachusetts Audubon

xii

| Suitable for Young Children | Charles Canoe Access | Dogs Allowed | Street Access | Acres | Scenic Vista | Rocky Ledge | Area Manager |
|---|---|---|---|---|---|---|---|
| ✔ | ✔ | ✔ | Causeway St. | 225 | | | T |
| ✔ | | ✔ | Noon Hill St. | 204 | ✔ | ✔ | T |
| | ✔ | ✔ | Charles St. | 150 | ✔ | ✔ | T |
| ✔ | ✔ | ✔ | Route 27 | 150 | ✔ | ✔ | T |
| ✔ | ✔ | ✔ | Bridge St. | 91 | | | T |
| ✔ | ✔ | | Route 16 | 608 | | | A |
| ✔ | ✔ | ✔ | Route 16 | 182 | | | MDC |
| ✔ | | ✔ | Dedham St. | 591 | ✔ | ✔ | T |
| ✔ | ✔ | ✔ | Canoe Access off Fisher St. | 29 | ✔ | | T |
| ✔ | | ✔ | Common St. | 200 | ✔ | ✔ | MDC |
| ✔ | | ✔ | Central Ave. | 23 | ✔ | ✔ | MDC |

MDC=Metropolitan District Commision

# MAP KEY

—————  Road

~~~  River

▬  Lake or pond

▓▓▓▓  Dam

– – – –  Walk/bike path

▬  Canoe access and parking

🚲  Beginning of bike route

▬▬▬  Bike route

✗  Wildlife viewing

⌂  Boat house

# 1

## The Source

I STARTED EXPLORING the Charles twenty years ago merely as a way to enjoy a day on the water. I wanted to spend some time away from the sprawl of suburban development, and the Upper Charles seemed like one of the few places left that was not privately owned. The river didn't disappoint me; it was quiet, rich in wildlife, and, best of all, easily accessible. There are no Keep Out signs on the Charles; its beauty is available to all. Yet, surprisingly, I encountered no other canoeists on that first trip, and I felt the thrill of the explorer who discovers something new.

At first, the strokes of the paddle, the colors of the river, and the variety of the shoreline were enough to keep me happy. But the river has power. Not the power of its current, but the power of wonder—even now, it pulls me along, beckoning me to further exploration.

Each trip on the river left me with more questions than answers. Was the fishing good? Were there any rapids? What was the upper river like? And, ultimately, where was the source? Weekends were no longer my own; they belonged to the river. Each year I focused on a different aspect of the Charles. I spent that first year canoeing different stretches and discovering favorite spots. The next year, I tracked and observed a herd of deer that lived along the river in its middle reaches. I began taking wildlife and landscape photos as well. I was constantly shooting pictures of the river in all its seasons, in all its moods. I spent hours, telephoto lens at hand, waiting patiently for an otter or a great blue heron to pose for my idea of the "perfect" picture.

The fishing fever caught me when I first landed a four-pound largemouth bass. I fell into the trap that ensnares all anglers: the goal of trying to catch bigger and bigger fish, much the way a golfer is enslaved by trying to shoot better and better rounds. First, I searched for a lunker largemouth; then, later, I frustrated myself with the fly rod, angling for trout in the Norfolk-Millis area. But I reaped many rewards; during each outing, the river slowly revealed more of its secrets, charms, and surprises.

I've meandered in my pursuits in much the same manner as the river twists and turns for more than eighty miles. But while the Charles River finally makes it to the sea, I've seemed to come full circle. These days, I spend less time pursuing my river hobbies and more time simply canoeing for the sake of being on the water.

I tried to learn everything I could about the river, and the river in turn taught me the virtues of patience and observation. I soon realized that my best outings on the Charles were the times when I let the slow, dark waters of the river show me the way. Trips were more fruitful in terms of enjoying nature when I left my wristwatch at home and let the day unfold, rather than stick to any set plan or preconceived notions. Nature truly does reveal itself in subtle ways and on its own schedule.

It wasn't until I bought a house near the headwaters of the Charles that I wondered about its source. The Charles's origin proved to be yet another surprise—the source remains a mystery.

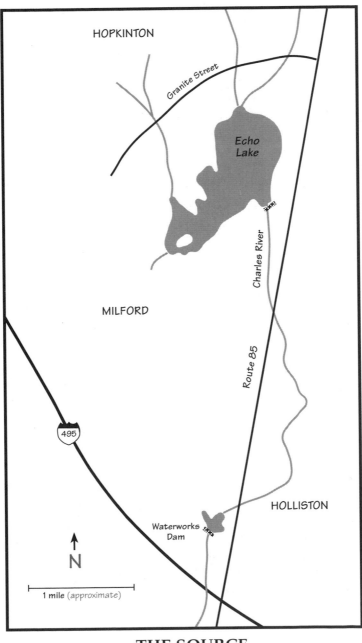

**THE SOURCE**

Echo Lake in Hopkinton is the official source of the Charles, but Echo Lake is a man-made body of water, and I do not consider this the river's natural origin. Created in 1884 by the Milford Water Company, Echo Lake was built to supply water for the towns of Milford and Hopedale. The spot was chosen because the slopes surrounding this upper portion of the Charles were steep and rocky, perfect for creating a reservoir. Only the northern reaches of the pond have a gentle slope where the feeder streams enter. The granite ledges in the area provided the necessary material for dam construction, thereby keeping masonry costs to a minimum. The convex shape of the dam was something of a novelty at the time, but the design was a sound one—the dam has stood for more than 110 years.

Echo Lake is a scenic little lake, but privately owned. (I secured permission from the Milford Water Company to view the lake for my river research.) However, you can follow the Charles a short distance after it exits Echo Lake by searching for a little brook tumbling over the rocks along Route 85, just to the east of Route 495. That brook is the Charles.

This small flow of water was hardly what the early explorers had envisioned. Captain John Smith, upon seeing the wide mouth of the Charles, assumed it to be a great river, heading far inland. Apparently, so did England's Prince Charles; thinking the river to be a tremendous waterway, he modestly named the river after himself in 1615.

The first explorers never imagined that the Charles meanders every which way, narrowing considerably in inland reaches. Although the river is eighty miles long, it does not flow from the heart of the country—its headwaters are only about twenty-eight miles from Boston as the crow flies. Certainly, the Charles is not on the scale of the Hudson or the Connecticut River, but its size is perfect for the modern-day explorer who wonders what's around the next bend.

The Indians got it right—they called the river Quinobequin, meaning "circular." They knew the river as a partner. It was their highway and their supermarket, an integral part of their daily lives, providing for many of their needs. Even today, the river serves as one of the last wildlife corridors in the area.

Indian camps were scattered all along the Charles, usually at the river's confluence with major tributaries or adjacent ponds, such as South End Pond in Millis. High ground next to the river was favored by Indians to avoid both flooding and mosquitoes. Other popular spots for camps were near stretches of rapids or waterfalls, where spawning fish could easily be speared or caught in weirs.

The earliest known inhabitants of the Charles were the Paleo-Indians, who moved northward into the region more than 10,000 years ago. The second group of inhabitants, called the Algonquians or Algonkins, settled in Massachusetts from 2,000 to 3,000 years ago, and separate tribes were formed according to the regions each settled. The Wampanoags lived in the south coastal area, while the Massachusetts tribe settled in what is now the greater Boston area, and the Nipmucks settled in central Massachusetts and along the upper reaches of the Charles.

Many of us think of Indians as nomads, but these eastern American Indians cultivated small plots of land, growing corn and squashes along the coast and in the fertile river valleys. They moved seasonally to hunt game, but each tribe had its own territory, and each smaller band had its own small farming plots. Their life was in harmony with their surroundings.

Early white settlers arrived with the idea of transforming the natural setting to suit their needs. Often the Charles was viewed as an opportunity ready to be exploited. Dams were built to supply free power for saw- and gristmills, to be followed later by paper, iron, and textile mills. When the river was seen as a nuisance, that, too, was reason for

*Echo Lake in Hopkinton—the official source of the Charles.*

altering its natural flow. In some instances, ditches were dug to drain the low-lying meadows to create more farmland. Examples of this practice can still be seen in the town of Dedham, where Long Ditch stretches for a half-mile and the man-made Mother Brook diverts water from the Charles to the nearby Neponset River. No matter what the reason for altering the river, little thought was given to long-term ramifications.

It's too bad the Indians could not have continued to manage the river. Long before the rock-and-roll song "Dirty Water" (by the Standells, 1960s) broadcast the river's sorry condition, the white man had been abusing the Charles. Early textile mills, followed by modern industry, then wastewater sewage—all contributed to polluting the river. Although the mills have since been abandoned, problems with pollution persist. But, there's been a vast improvement over the past twenty-five years. The Charles truly can be called an environmental success story, thanks to the efforts of a number of groups, including the Charles River Watershed Association.

The Charles River Watershed Association (CRWA) is comprised of people from all walks of life who share a common concern: the well-being of the Charles. It is a nonprofit organization established in 1965 whose mission is to "protect, improve, and expand the natural resources and recreational opportunities of the Charles River Watershed, and to enhance their enjoyment by the inhabitants."

The association is active in educating the public and recruiting volunteers to help the river. Its members give slide shows and workshops, publish a quarterly newsletter, maintain a resource library, and hold a variety of river-related events. Their most successful recreational event is the Run of the Charles, when approximately 2,000 paddlers gather each spring for a series of canoe and kayak races on the lower river.

*The beginning of the Charles, a clean, bubbling brook following Route 85 in Milford, just below Echo Lake.*

The association has much to be vigilant about: wetlands alterations, water withdrawals, sewer overflows, bridge construction and renovation, erosion control, and recreational-boating conflicts. These issues affect me directly—without a healthy river, I have no quiet place to escape, there will be no six-pound largemouth, and my perfect wildlife photo will forever remain just a wish.

The recreational potential of the Charles is enormous. I estimate that well over a million people live within a ten- or fifteen-minute drive to the river. The winding ways of the Charles result in some other impressive figures: It drains more than 309 square miles, has more than 20,000 acres of wetlands, and has twenty dams and more than ninety bridges. There are thirty-five towns in the Charles River watershed, and twenty-three of them have river frontage. Finally, the Charles has more than seventy feeder streams, some of which are canoeable.

The perception of the Charles as a city river is misleading. Most of the Charles flows through natural settings; some spots seem so remote, it's hard to believe they lie only a few miles from a major metropolitan area. And while the river may belong to "the People," only a fraction of them have given it more than a passing glance. In fact, that was the way I used to think of the river—I knew it was out there, but that was about it.

All that changed after my first few outings. I had grossly underrated the river's beauty. Visits had a mixture of both relaxation and excitement—but never boredom. Over the years, I began to understand why the Indians viewed the river as a partner.

# 2

## Twenty Miles on the Upper Charles

OR ME THE TRUE source of the Charles shall remain a mystery. It could be any one of the small brooks or springs that feed Echo Lake, which lies just to the east of Route 495. If you drive down Granite Street in Hopkinton, you can see a couple of these brooks; perhaps one of these is the real Charles.

Regardless of the exact starting point of the Charles, the headwaters are small indeed. As the river passes through Milford and Bellingham, it gathers a little strength and widens, although not much. Those who attempt to canoe here do as much walking as paddling. I recently explored this stretch of the river on a hot August day and found the "mighty Charles" reduced to a river of marsh grass passing through the occasional dam, pond, and low-lying woods. It didn't have the exceptional canoeing found just a few miles downstream, but it did have its own charm. There were spots of fast water around one bend and large swamps around the next. It's as if the river could not decide between being a mountain stream or a broad, flood-plain waterway.

Through Hopkinton, Milford, and western Bellingham, the primary flow of the river is southward, as if heading

*A "river of grass" on the Hopedale-Mendon-Bellingham line.*

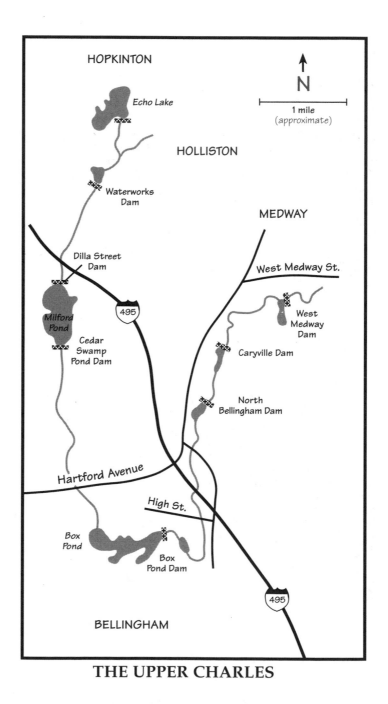

HOPKINTON

Echo Lake

N
1 mile
(approximate)

HOLLISTON

Waterworks
Dam

MEDWAY

Dilla Street
Dam

West Medway St.

495

West
Medway
Dam

Milford
Pond

Cedar
Swamp
Pond Dam

Caryville Dam

North
Bellingham Dam

Hartford Avenue

High St.

Box
Pond

Box
Pond Dam

495

BELLINGHAM

# THE UPPER CHARLES

toward Providence, Rhode Island. Then, after exiting Box Pond in Bellingham, the river turns in a northerly direction, where it once again passes under Route 495. I've done a bit of fishing in the Bellingham stretch, and although it's not as productive as a stretch farther downriver, I've caught a few bass. The river has more than twenty species of fish and, God knows, I've given every one of them my best effort. Over time, I've found a few hot spots. Some of these I'll discuss, but there are a couple of others I won't share with even my best friends. We anglers are a secretive lot. I'm sure my secret spots are probably the secret spots of a few other fishermen, and more than likely these coveted areas are probably little better than the next turn in the river. But we all need special places to call our own.

The flowage through North Bellingham, Medway, and Franklin is canoeable in high water, but I would not advise it, especially if you are interested in a lengthy outing without portaging. Novice canoers should avoid the area due to the many dams and obstructions in the water. Kayakers will find the going a bit easier, but they will still have to portage around the many dams. Compared to a few miles downstream, access is poor, and I've only done some spot canoeing here. You'll find, however, if you do a bit of exploring, pockets of secluded woods where an hour's trip is worthwhile. I can recall a nice paddle along the river near Bent Street in Franklin, where I spotted two red-tailed hawks lazily circling. They stayed high, effortlessly riding a thermal, rarely even flapping their impressive, outstretched wings.

Through the Medway-Franklin area, the Charles begins to look like a river rather than a stream. Feeder brooks add to its current and depth. Greenish brown is the river's predominant color, giving it an Amazonian appearance—I almost expect to see an alligator sunning on the banks. Traveling due east now, the Charles makes a quiet entrance into Populatic Pond, a small, shallow body of water, and the many houses and cottages dotting its shoreline stand in contrast to the more secluded Charles. I consider this the end of the "small Charles" and the beginning of the "big Charles." When the river exits the pond at the west end, it gets wider and deeper and seems to really mean business.

Prime canoeing, fishing, and wildlife observation can be found in this next stretch, as the Charles heads northeasterly, appearing to make a direct course to Boston. But, fortunately, the river's tendency to meander again takes it through some of the most scenic areas in New England.

One June morning, I followed the beckoning current and let the river gently carry me out of Populatic Pond. The Charles seemed to flow through a tunnel of green, as the overhanging foliage blocked out a good deal of the sun. Passing from open pond to the intimate confines of the stream heightened my sense of adventure. Perhaps today I would catch a six-pound bass.

I had loaded my one-seater Old Town Pack canoe with a variety of fishing tackle, and at first the thirteen-foot vessel felt too small to handle the river. This was the canoe's maiden voyage, and I was a bit concerned—a short section of rapids lay ahead. The Pack canoe was purchased for a variety of reasons, the primary one being that it was light enough for one person to carry easily and lift onto the top of a car. It is made of lightweight plastics that are more durable than wood, aluminum, and fiberglass. As an extra bonus, its small size makes for easier paddling and quicker maneuverability—important features when navigating a river with more than a few obstructions.

Before long, I adjusted to the canoe's size, and it proved more than capable. I was content to drift along slowly, with an occasional stroke more for direction than speed. The Charles follows an easterly course here, roughly paralleling River Road in Norfolk. A couple of years earlier, a friend of mine caught a six-pound largemouth bass along this stretch. He was actually going after trout and was equipped with fairly light tackle when the fish hit. Only beginner's luck

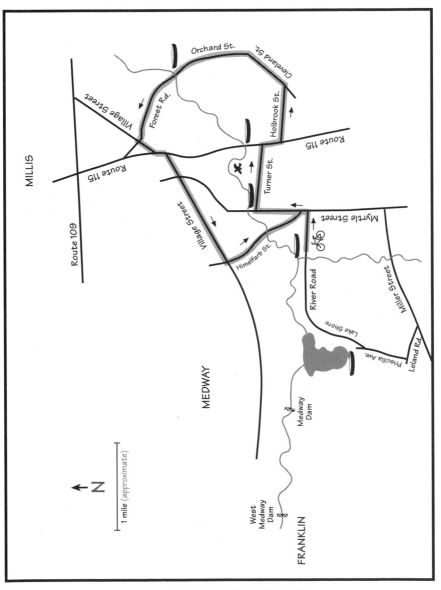

**FRANKLIN TO MILLIS**

*A marsh in Bellingham.*

could account for the fact that his four-pound-test line held during a ten-minute battle of epic proportions. Unfortunately, I was downstream and missed the fight, but I did see the bass—a very fat fish with an enormous head.

Floating down the river, I had my friend's bass in mind, and I dropped anchor directly across from a large, partially submerged tree. Casting a rubber worm next to the tangle of branches, I settled back against the stern. No strikes came as I bounced the lure along, but my eye caught a movement beyond the fallen tree. Standing in three inches of water was a great blue heron.

If the bird had not moved, I never would have picked out its slate gray silhouette from the riverbank. Apparently my close proximity made it nervous, and after another second, with extended wings, it pushed off. It appeared as if the heron's bulk would impede its flight, but with two great flaps of its wings awkwardness was replaced by grace. Silently, this bird, which seemed strangely prehistoric to me, headed downstream. Massive wings, long neck, and trailing legs made an impressive sight as the heron followed the river's course and escaped my presence. Long after it vanished, I sat and marveled over how large these birds really are.

The bass didn't cooperate, so I lifted anchor and continued downstream, passing by Mill River on my right (right or left references are always made in the context of facing downstream). On prior outings, I had canoed this brook during high water. For most of its length, it passes through marshland, where a variety of ducks and turtles can be seen.

Mill River has a few deep holes that allow a limited number of stocked trout to "hold over" and flourish season after season. I've caught brook trout here in late March, long before the first hatchery trucks deliver the initial allotment of fish. Native trout are another matter; the Mill River is simply too warm in the summer to support a thriving brookie population. However, farther along the Charles, there are a handful of feeder streams that have a small population of natives.

These fish cannot tolerate pollution, and, while their habitat has certainly diminished, it's encouraging to know they survive in a few hidden forest streams. Small feeder streams usually provide a better environment for trout than does the Charles, because they flow through more shady areas, thereby keeping the water cooler. Streams also tend to have more rocky areas, where the quick water becomes oxygenated.

The warm-water fish population has fared even better during the past twenty years. All along the Charles, I've noticed a steady improvement in the bass fishing, which I confirmed in a conversation with Walter Hoyt, Northeast District manager for the Massachusetts Division of Fisheries and Wildlife. Hoyt told me, "The warm-water species have been doing quite well over the last few years; food sources are increasing and water quality has improved."

While the river's fish habitat remains strong, another development threatens nearby vegetation and wildlife. A purple-colored weed, called purple loosestrife, is spreading at an alarming pace throughout the low-lying areas of the Northeast and Midwest. The lance-shaped weed can grow as tall as four feet, and before I learned of its detrimental effects, I would admire its vivid purple flowers, seen throughout the summer. Purple loosestrife is not indigenous to America; the seeds were carried here from Europe in the late 1700s or early 1800s, and by 1810 the plant had established itself in Massachusetts.

The banks of the Charles and Sudbury Rivers have thick stands of loosestrife, and without American predators it is growing out of control. It is feared that wildlife will suffer, because loosestrife is low in nutritional value compared to the native plants it is crowding out. Efforts to eradicate it have failed. Researchers have tried mowing the plants, only to have more-numerous shoots grow. A possible solution might be to introduce a European beetle that attacks the plant; entomologists must first be sure the beetles will not eat native plants as well. Studies are currently being conducted by the University of Massachusetts and the Massachusetts Audubon Society.

Two other nonindigenous plants causing problems on the river are milfoil and water chestnut. Experimental treatment for the milfoil (a submerged plant) was attempted on the Charles with herbicides but proved successful for only a year or two before the plant came back as strong as ever. Controlling the water chestnut has met with somewhat better results through mechanical harvesting. Individuals can help control the spread of both weeds by cleaning their boat bottoms and propellers so as not to introduce the weed to other ponds, and by limiting use of fertilizers and detergents, which leach phosphorus into the river and promote the growth of these nonnative weeds.

Don't confuse these weeds with the native duckweed, a tiny floating plant that often forms a carpet over the surface of the Charles. The yellow-green fronds are only one-sixteenth to three-eighths of an inch in size and are especially relished by waterfowl.

Beside the non-indigenous plants, another man-made threat to the river is water draw-off. As the suburbs along the Charles grow in population, the number of wells near the river or along its tributaries have increased in alarming proportion. Two new wells in operation at Elm Bank Reservation received considerable attention, but there are several others upstream that also tap the aquifers. Kate Bowditch, Environmental Affairs coordinator for the Charles River Watershed Association told me in 1997 that eight new wells were currently in the permitting process and more were sure to follow. Bowditch correctly points out that water draw-off is often harder to regulate than direct pollution into the river. While the Clean Water Act of 1972 clearly regulates discharges, the law that addresses river flow and volume is not nearly as clear and lacks the teeth of the Clean Water Act.

"The problem is cumulative," said Bowditch. "Each well is tapping aquifers that normally contribute water to

*From marsh to quickwater, Bellingham-Mendon.*

the Charles. Low flow, combined with an increase in effluent discharges, will seriously affect the health of the Charles. It will make it difficult for the river to handle the treated effluent that enters from various sources. The sewage treatment plant that services Medway, Millis, Franklin, Norfolk, and Bellingham wants to increase its discharge by 25 percent, which will only add to the problem."

As I paddled downstream past the Mill River during that June outing, I approached a few rapids. These are not Allagash River–type rapids, but I have seen a couple of canoes flip here. Although there is little actual whitewater and the river itself isn't all that deep, the current quickens as the main channel narrows. And negotiating under the Myrtle Street bridge and around the bridge pilings can be tricky. Perhaps the biggest threat is from the boulders submerged just below the surface.

One early-spring morning, I was fishing from shore near these rapids. A group of father-and-son teams shot by in canoes. The last pair to go by took a different channel than the others and promptly grounded themselves on a boulder. It appeared that the rock was directly under the boat, and paddle as they might, the twosome could not budge the canoe. Then they tried rocking the boat. Big mistake. It capsized immediately, spilling father, son, and all their gear into the icy current. Fortunately, they were wearing life jackets and were able to half swim, half walk to shore.

I always remember that mishap when I paddle this area, so I put on my life jacket. As I approached the bridge, the side I prefer to pass under was blocked by a fallen tree; I had no choice but to shoot through the other side. The little Pack canoe picked up speed and then came to a grinding halt. I, too, was hung up on rocks. Unlike the swollen, muddy conditions of early spring, however, the water now was quite shallow. All I had to do was step out of the canoe and gently slide it a yard or two downstream.

Still in most seasons, the water level in this Norfolk-Millis stretch is high enough for canoes to move right along, rarely touching bottom. Late spring and early summer are especially good, as the water level is still high after the early spring runoff. However, during dry periods, often in late summer and fall, expect some low-water spots—usually under the bridges. Don't let this deter you during the autumn, as the colorful scenery more than makes up for shallow channels. Peak foliage season usually comes a bit earlier along the river than elsewhere; the many swamp maples are the first to explode with shades of red and yellow.

After freeing myself from the rocks, I enjoyed a fast run of water before the current dropped me into a large pool just below the Myrtle Street bridge. Skunk cabbage, tall weeds, and cedars lined the pool, and ahead lay the remains of an old stone bridge. I could see a curious mix of both new and old houses through the trees. It's easy to discern the old houses, with their nearby barns and lichen-covered stone walls, from the newer ones, which usually have large glass windows over-looking the river. The occasional canoe or rowboat lying by the water's edge told me these riverbank homeowners enjoy not only viewing the river, but spending time on it as well.

Where the river makes a sharp right turn, I spotted a huge snapping turtle lying half out of the water on the bank. I estimated its weight to be twenty pounds, and I have no doubt the river has snappers almost twice that size. Spotting one of these snappers is difficult indeed, since its shell looks just like a rock covered with moss. Snappers are feared by many people, but they go about their business (usually at night) with little or no contact with humans, and surely they have as much right to the river as any of us.

As I watched the old turtle, I could feel the river tug-ging at my canoe. Passing beneath the Pleasant Street bridge was a bit tricky, but the narrow channels were deep enough to run. I maneuvered toward the right bank and pulled out for the day.

The next morning my longtime fishing companion, Jon Cogswell, and I were on the river at dawn in my two-man,

*Quickwater below Myrtle Street bridge (Norfolk-Millis).*

fifteen-foot Coleman canoe. This vessel is heavier than the little Old Town Pack canoe because of its extra size and steel parts. But its tough plastic shell is flexible and can really take a beating—a good feature when Jon and I canoe. We spend more time fishing than paddling and have learned the hard way that canoes don't have brakes. Once when Jon and I were on the Charles, I hooked a two- or three-pound bass, and while I played the fish, Jon grabbed the net, leaving the canoe at the mercy of the current. The canoe did a slow 360-degree turn and, with the aid of a boulder, severed my fishing line. A bystander on a nearby bridge had a good laugh as our canoe continued sideways down the river.

Cogs and I launched just below the Pleasant Street bridge in Millis, and as soon as we rounded the first bend a great blue heron gave a couple of loud squawks and took flight. I thought perhaps its nest was nearby, but Wayne Petersen, a field ornithologist with the Massachusetts Audubon Society, told me the bird was probably just hunting. Petersen said that most of the great blue herons breeding in Massachusetts do so in secluded beaver ponds. Perhaps the best site to view a heron rookery (from a safe distance, so as not to disturb them) is at the head of the Assabet River in Westborough.

The great blue heron population has dramatically increased in Massachusetts during recent years, and I often see herons on the Charles, especially in the spring. Reduced pollution in rivers and lakes is the primary reason for their success—cleaner waters mean more fish, and herons have voracious appetites. A 1996 survey conducted by the Massachusetts Division of Fisheries and Wildlife says that there are 63 known nesting areas in the state with 716 active nests. This is a dramatic increase over the 38 nesting areas recorded in a 1989 survey. Most of the sites are located in the central part of the state, and the great majority are built in standing timber flooded by beaver dams. It seems the beaver are as important to the herons as clean water, providing them with

*Norfolk & Millis Dean Street area.*

safe nesting areas where raccoons, a chief predator of fledglings and eggs, are thwarted by the water they must cross to reach the nests. (Surprisingly, there are a few nests built in upland timber, without any surrounding water.) The closest heronry to the Charles is in Norfolk, in an upstream section of the Stop River. Staff members of the Stony Brook Wildlife Sanctuary in Norfolk lead occasional trips to the heronry, where one can see the herons coming and going from nests in the constant effort of securing food for their young.

Tom French, a wildlife biologist with the Massachusetts Division of Fisheries and Wildlife, explained to me that although great blue herons are seen feeding along coastal areas, they always nest inland. This is just the opposite of the black-crowned night heron; these tend to nest on islands in Boston Harbor, then move up the Charles for feeding. Tom and I discussed other wildlife along the Charles, like the peregrine falcons nesting at the Christian Science building that use the open space above the Charles for soaring and hunting.

A not-so-welcome addition to the Charles is the European rudd, an exotic fish that looks like a golden shiner. This nonnative fish is the only exotic in the Charles, and was introduced to the river when it was used as live bait for fishing. When the Division of Fisheries and Wildlife learned that the fish was used as bait, they tightened regulations that limit bait fish to native fish or fish that have been in the river for so long they cannot do any additional damage.

Tom and I speculated that a future visitor to the Charles could also be the largest—the moose. Its population is rising dramatically in New England as farms revert back to forest. Although most people think that moose are only in northern New England, Massachusetts has approximately fifty resident moose in the state, and possibly as many as a hundred. These are not just the young males passing through, but breeding pairs and young. In 1996 a female was killed by a car in Sterling, which is not all that far from the Charles. So next time you round a bend on the river, keep your nerves steady and your canoe stable if you spot something the size of a horse quietly feeding in the shallows.

Jon remarked how wonderful it was to see wildlife so close to the greater Boston area. His comment reminded me of similar observations made by Larry McCarthy, a former member of the Charles River Watershed Association's board of directors. His enthusiasm for the Charles is evident whenever we compare river notes. In a recent conversation, he summed up the comeback of the Charles: "The river has become a vibrant ecosystem once again, and the Charles is known as a national environmental success story."

It was only thirty years ago that the pollution on the river made it the butt of jokes, and few people harbored any hope for its improvement. Today most of the river, with the exception of the Charles River Basin, is clean enough for fishing, swimming, and wind surfing. And the Charles River Watershed Association and the state's Department of Environmental Protection have the common goal of making the basin a class B waterway (fishable/swimmable). While much of the river may be clean enough for swimming, its murky waters make it unsafe and swimming is actually prohibited. It's not wise to swim in any water where you cannot spot submerged logs and rocks. Today much of the river's dark coloring is caused by the natural release of tannin from vegetation.

It's easy to feel a sense of ownership when canoeing the river, and often, if I'm driving by, I stop to check on "my" river, to see how it's doing. This feeling of proprietorship is especially strong when I'm canoeing downstream in the Upper Charles and suddenly notice how quiet things are. The stillness leads me to imagine I am the first person to travel this stretch of water, a Captain Smith of eastern Massachusetts. The landscape along the river hasn't really changed much since the days of the Indians, and it's easy to let my imagination run free. That's the beauty of canoeing: I can pass through the heart of otherwise impenetrable swamps and marshlands where human hands have not altered the terrain. And the fact that the Upper Charles is relatively narrow and shallow provides an extra bonus—no powerboats or jet skis. On the upper Charles, the only wake I encounter is that of a muskrat, and the only buzz, the soothing sound of crickets.

Jon and I passed two large maples on our right that looked so inviting we decided to stop. We sat down and poured cups of coffee from the thermos, and while we relaxed, I related another sorry tale about the one that got away. A month earlier, just as dusk was yielding to night, I was angling for bass on the river when a tremendous fish slammed my lure. It took awhile to work the bass to within five feet of me, and by that time it was very dark. I had gotten only a glimpse of its outline. Without a net (a trout net never would have handled this fish, anyway), my only option was to try to beach it. I certainly wasn't going to reach down into the black water and grab it; more than likely I'd have had a Rapala minnow lure embedded in my hand. Slowly, I worked the fish toward shore, and just as I thought I really might be able to slide it up onto the bank, the bass felt the bottom and, in a spray of water, snapped the line with a violent roll.

Jon and I had better luck soon after we finished our coffee. Instead of bass, we each caught a trout. Both were beautiful, iridescent-colored rainbows about fourteen inches long. Even when Jon and I don't catch anything, we have the enjoyment of the river. Thoreau said it best: "Commonly they did not think that they were lucky or well paid for their time unless they got a long string of fish, though they had the opportunity of seeing the pond all the while."

The Charles receives a healthy stocking of trout each spring in the towns of Norfolk, Millis, Dover, and Natick. Although some nice-sized rainbows are stocked (and I love the leaps they make), I wish the river received all brown trout. Browns would be best suited to the warm, slow waters of the Charles.

*Passing beneath the Pleasant Street bridge was a bit tricky (Norfolk-Millis).*

Jon and I packed our trout in the cooler and continued our downstream journey. Around the bend, we were greeted by wide, sunny banks and grazing cows. I've long considered the area that borders Norfolk and Millis to be one of the most picturesque places on the whole river; the pastures and farmland offer a welcome vista after the prior stretch of dense woods. Jon likes it for a different reason: the solitude. He can quietly work his fly rod without interruption from other anglers and devote his full concentration to the sport.

As usual, Jon and I were so engrossed in the fishing that we forgot to pay attention to what lay directly ahead. We made a direct hit on a submerged tree and almost capsized. The incident reminded me of a passage from an old book by James Schultz called *Floating Down the Missouri.* Written in 1901, it describes the hazards of fallen tree trunks: "If the tip is just beneath the surface, a swirl and rippling of water reveals its presence. But the most observant

*Anglers enjoy the slow current in a shallow reach of the Charles (Norfolk-Millis).*

pilots cannot always detect one, and with a crash, the boat is impaled and a few moments later sinks."

Fortunately the Charles is an easy river to navigate (provided one's paying attention). The current is so slow, except during heavy spring runoff or rains, that you have plenty of time to spot obstructions. Even if you do hit something, a gentle nudge will usually free the canoe—just avoid any sudden, jerky movements that could startle your partner.

Our canoe didn't sink, and, regaining our balance, we prepared to run the quick water below the Route 115 bridge. We did so without incident and were rewarded by seeing an otter searching for fish or crayfish near the riverbank. Otters are rare on the Charles, but every once in awhile I'm treated to a glimpse of one.

The beaver is another fur-bearing animal that spends most of its time in the water. Beaver were once populous all along the Charles and throughout Massachusetts, but around 1860 they disappeared from the state. A combination of unlimited trapping and the continued transformation of the land from forest to agricultural uses brought about the demise of the beaver. Trapping is now controlled, however, and many undeveloped areas are reverting to woodland. The beaver has been reintroduced to Massachusetts primarily through the efforts of the Division of Fisheries and Wildlife. Tom Decker, a biologist with that agency, told me that the beaver are now doing quite well in Massachusetts. The Charles has had an occasional beaver in the watershed, but they are not as populous there as in watersheds just to the north of the Massachusetts Turnpike and to the west of Route 495. But it's just a matter of time before the beavers are again well established in the Charles. The Upper Charles offers excellent habitat for beaver with its many broad, secluded marshes and feeder streams.

Shortly beyond Route 115, a large solitary boulder can be seen on the right. Perhaps it was brought here by a glacier during the Ice Age, more than 10,000 years ago. Whenever I

*Fishing by Forest Road (Millis-Medfield).*

see this huge rock, I imagine a tall Indian standing on its top, silently surveying the river's activity. (Samuel de Champlain recorded that the Indians of New England were taller than Europeans.) At night along the river, I can picture Indians gathered around a great fire on the bank, roasting chunks of venison. Deer were plentiful in these parts, and the Indians found a use for the entire animal—organs, meat, skin, bones, antlers. Waste of an animal's body would be a sign of disrespect to its spirit.

Jon and I continued our paddle through meadows and woods, eventually taking out at Forest Road in Millis. To stretch our legs, we took a walk west along this road, lined with stone walls, fields, and houses well over a hundred years old. We'd had a good day on the Charles and I felt refreshed. Maybe the soothing greens and browns of the river and its scenery have a calming effect. Again I thought of Thoreau: "Let us spend one day as deliberately as Nature and not be thrown off the track by every nutshell and mosquito's wing that falls on the rails."

# First Twenty Miles

## PADDLING

### Populatic Pond and Upstream

From a launch site on River Road in Norfolk, paddle upstream toward Populatic Pond. There is good largemouth bass fishing among the fallen trees that line the bank. After a short distance (about a mile) you will reach the pond, and if you hug the northern bank, you will see where the Charles enters it. The river is noticeably smaller and narrower here, but it still can be explored by canoe. You can view a small marsh area by traveling upstream. When you are ready to return, simply let the current carry you back to your car.

### Downstream from Populatic Pond

*One Car:* If you are canoeing alone and have only one car, I would suggest putting in at Forest Road on the Millis-Medfield border. I like to go upstream first; that way you get the hard work over with and, when you're ready to return, just turn around and let the current bring you back to your car. This stretch is mostly wooded and has some shallow water upstream.

*Two Cars:* Leave one car at Forest Road and drive upstream all the way to the intersection of Turner and Dean Streets in Norfolk. You can park on Turner Street, carry your canoe a few yards through the woods, and put in just below the quick water that shoots under the bridge. You will pass through a combination of woods, then farm fields, then woods again. This is a secluded stretch of river, and you will pass under only one road (Route 115).

*Caught one!*

There are some low-water spots and an occasional obstruction, but the trip is well worth the effort. About three miles; no portages.

# RIVER WALKS
## Populatic Pond and Upstream

To see the headwaters of the Charles, try taking a stroll along Granite Street in Hopkinton, a quiet residential road that lies at the northern end of Echo Lake. Any one of the feeder streams you pass might be the source of the Charles.

Another quiet street worth exploring is High Street in Bellingham. A long marsh runs from south to north, with the Charles flowing through its heart in the same direction. A nice spot for seeing ducks and birds.

## Downstream from Populatic Pond

Forest Road, heading west, is a beautiful old New England road with fields, stone walls, pine forest, and houses from the eighteenth and nineteenth centuries.

# BIKING

This eight-mile loop ride through Millis, Norfolk, and Medfield follows back roads that receive little traffic and passes by a couple of farms near the Charles. The outing starts on River Road where there is shoulder parking near where the Mill River spills into the Charles. Follow River Road to the east 0.1 mile to its intersection with Myrtle Street and go left for a hundred yards to where the road forks. Bear right here onto Dean Street and proceed 0.4 mile to Turner Street on the right. (You might want to get off your bike and walk up to the narrow bridge on Dean Street for view of the Charles, where rapids surge below in the high water of spring. In the autumn this is a scenic spot with the colorful foliage of swamp maples draping over the river. There is a dry, grassy bank alongside the river hidden in the woods located on the south side of the river and reached by a muddy foot trail from Turner Street just a hundred yards downstream from the bridge.)

Our ride continues on Turner Street, which turns into Holbrook Street. Go 0.7 mile down this wooded lane until you reach Route 115, and then ride to the right for 0.2 mile until you see the other side of Holbrook Street on your left. Follow the hills of Holbrook Street for 0.8 mile, and then go left on Cleveland Street for 0.9 mile until you come to Fruit Street on your left. Take Fruit Street by the beautiful fields of Paul and Jane's Farm (good birding) and travel out of Norfolk into Medfield. Fruit Street turns into Orchard Street and crosses the Charles at 1.3 miles from where you first entered these roads. This is a secluded stretch of river that passes through thick woods; for those who like an intimate paddle in the shade, this is the spot. When you cross the river the road becomes Forest Street, and you should pedal uphill about 0.8 mile to the intersection of Village Street and turn left. Proceed for 0.5 mile to where Village Street merges with Route 115 and go straight. Our trip then turns to the right where Village Street splits from Route 115 after just 0.2 mile, but you may want to pedal ahead a short distance to the Route 115 bridge, where there is a farm along the riverbank to the right and quick water on the left side of the road.

We continue down Village Street 1.8 miles from where we entered from Forest Road (some traffic at rush hour) to Himelfarb Street on the left. Take Himelfarb Street, a quiet wooded back road, 0.8 mile to a bridge over the Charles with a nice run of quick water. Then turn right on Myrtle Street and proceed 100 yards to River Road on your right, where the trip began. You can extend your outing by following River Road and the other back roads past Populatic Pond to Miller Street and making a small loop back to your car.

## BIRDING

Typically the best birding on the river is along the open marshes, which attract a wide assortment of birds and water-fowl. These open areas often allow the best vantage points because there are few trees obstructing your line of sight. The greatest period of migration (which also provides the best birding opportunities) occurs from mid-April to early June and from late August to mid-November. These also happen to be great paddling times; not too cold and not too hot, with plenty of water in the Charles. Roughly 450 bird species have been sighted in Massachusetts, but only 300 are seen on a regular basis. Still, that is a lot of birds! About 60 of these are here year-round, 115 are summer visitors, and roughly 75 species are migrants. My favorite birding months on the Charles are May and September, with plenty of migrant birds passing through, crisp mornings for paddling, and generally pleasant, warm afternoons.

Near the headwaters of the Charles, the stretch of river running north and south of Hartford Avenue offers good birding through a narrow strip of marsh. Waterfowl, swal-lows, hawks, and marsh birds can be found here. Farther down the river, I enjoy birding in a stretch of the Charles that runs from Dean Street on the Norfolk-Millis line to Route 115. The river winds through a combination of woods, small marshy setbacks, and agricultural fields. Some of the more interesting birds I see here are the woodcock, wood duck, broad-winged hawk, great blue heron, and bluebird.

## ANGLING

Good largemouth bass fishing all over the river, including tributaries such as the Stop River, Bogastow Brook, Mill River, and South End Pond. Carp are scattered throughout the river. Pickerel are in the Great Marsh and South End Pond. Trout are stocked in Millis, Norfolk, and Medfield: try Forest Road in Medfield, Myrtle Street in Norfolk-Millis,

River Road in Norfolk, Route 115 in Norfolk-Millis, Mill River on Miller Street in Norfolk, and Bogastow Brook in Millis.

## PICNICKING

Waites Mill Park near the Dean and Pleasant Street bridge.

## POINTS OF HISTORIC INTEREST

The Millis Historical Society has laid out signs along the Millis Historical Trail (mostly along Route 115) that mark such points of interest as the Richardson house which had a tunnel leading from the house into the woods, thought to be used as an escape route during Indian attack and later as a hiding place in the Underground Railroad.

# 3

# The
# Great Marsh

## Forest Road, Millis, to Route 109, Medfield

ALTHOUGH THE DOWNSTREAM VIEW from Forest Road is of heavy timber, marshland is only a quarter-mile downstream. This is the beginning of the huge Millis-Medfield Marsh. I've spent quite a bit of time poking around this area, yet each trip brings a new surprise. Thoreau had similar experiences during a week-long trip down the Concord and Merrimack Rivers with his brother John in 1839. He was drawn to the water and described some of the natural wonders awaiting river-goers: "They shall see teal, blue-winged, green-winged shilldrake whistlers, black ducks, ospreys, and many other wild and noble sights before night, such as they who sit in parlors never dream of."

On my latest trip downstream from Forest Road, I saw an enormous dark-colored bird, just as impressive as those Thoreau recorded. Watching the bird, with its six-foot wingspan, soar high above the river, I guessed it was either an immature bald eagle or an immature turkey vulture. Before I could get a really good look at it through my binoculars, a crow came along and harassed the bird, chasing it away. The next day I spoke with an ornithologist at the Audubon

*The great Millis-Medfield Marsh.*

Society, who told me I had probably seen a turkey vulture in its spring migration north.

Like Thoreau, rivers have always fascinated me—as a nine-year-old in Longmeadow, Massachusetts, I would ride down neighborhood streams with my brother in a four-foot plastic boat. To a couple of imaginative young minds, our stream could have been the Mississippi, even though the current sent us through culverts under suburban roads. Later, as we gained more freedom, we would go down to the "meadows," which were vast wetlands abutting the Connecticut River. These forays to the meadows proved to be a great training ground for future exploration of the Charles. We would fish for the huge carp trapped in small pools after the swollen Connecticut receded in late spring.

The Charles has its share of the "lowly" carp, and in the shallow waters near Forest Road I once watched a half-dozen of these monsters spawn—one even bumped my canoe like a torpedo in slow motion.

The carp may be considered a trash fish, but I'm certainly not the first person to be intrigued by these behemoths, which can weigh in excess of twenty-five pounds. While reading *Fisherman's Bounty*, a treasure of angling lore edited by Nick Lyons, I happened upon a Charles River story written in 1955 by Leslie P. Thompson. He tells of an eighteen-pound carp he caught at "Medfield Meadows, Charles River." After landing the brute, he describes how another angler walked over and proposed a toast with a bit of spirits because "something should be done about this." Even today, I find that the Charles softens people, and strangers often exchange greetings and information as they canoe by. And I have always felt that anglers are the easiest folks to strike up a conversation with. They will readily share local fishing tips with a stranger, so long as they're not pressed to reveal the best spot—we all have our secrets.

Carp are not the only wild creatures in this area. On three different occasions I've seen deer along the river between Forest Road and the mouth of the Stop River. When I told a friend about this, he said, "Sure, and there're mountain lions in Dover, right?" So the next time I canoed this stretch, I brought my video camera along to capture proof. I thought that luck was with me, because as I rounded a corner a nice-sized doe was feeding not ten feet from the riverbank. Before she bolted, I was able to get a quick shot; upon returning home, however, the tape told a different story. A jumpy picture showed nothing but the river, trees, and sky. It's a good thing I'm not a hunter.

A little beyond Forest Road, on the east side of the Charles, lies the Shattuck Reservation, owned and operated by The Trustees of Reservations. The 225-acre reservation encompasses woodlands, meadows, and three small islands.

The organization was established in 1891 to "preserve beautiful and historic places for the use and enjoyment of the public." Charles Eliot of Boston, a young landscape architect, was the visionary who recognized the public's

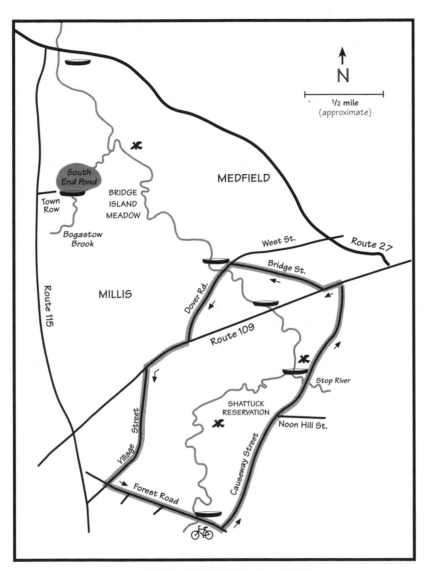

**THE GREAT MARSH**

need for open space. Today, The Trustees of Reservations owns and manages seventy-seven reservations totaling more than 20,000 acres, many of which are within the Charles River watershed. The Shattuck Reservation was a gift of Henry L. Shattuck in 1970, with thirteen acres given as a life estate by Robert I. Hunneman in 1978. The reservation protects one of the wildest areas on the river.

Directly across from the Shattuck Reservation, on the other side of Causeway Street, is another impressive area of conservation land called the Noon Hill Reservation, also owned by the Trustees. This rocky hill offers a good view of Medfield and Walpole to the east and south. At the base of Noon Hill is Holt Pond, where there's a good hiking trail. The whole area is worth exploring by foot.

On the west side of the river are a few houses close to an old bridge abutment where the river narrows (this can be a tricky spot). I would suspect that the folks in these houses have a real love for the Charles and probably know the river well. A friend of mine who lives farther down Causeway Street tells me that here the Charles overflows its banks almost every spring, closing a portion of Causeway Street. Rivers make moody, but interesting, neighbors.

While this area of the Charles is one of my favorites, I'm sobered whenever I pass the mouth of the Stop River, a major tributary seven miles long, which receives wastewater discharges from the Norfolk and Cedar Junction State Prisons. The Stop River is wide enough for canoeing, although one can never see more than a few feet ahead because of its many twists through the tall marsh grass. I've always wondered about the two oddly named islands in the Stop River Marsh: Childs Island and Devilsfoot Island. Devilsfoot Island apparently was named for strange depressions found in the island's rocks many years ago.

Medfield is one of those early New England towns that can get a history buff's juices flowing. In my opinion, the most exciting event in its history was the attack launched by

*Ruffed grouse chick in the leaves.*

Indians on Medfield in 1676. King Philip, whose Indian name was Metacom and who was leader of Wampanoag tribe, was one of the first Indians to recognize that further encroachment by the whites meant the Indian way of life was doomed. It is ironic that King Philip's father was Massasoit, the chief responsible for keeping the peace with the

Pilgrims in Plymouth. Philip knew that peace would result in additional expansion by the settlers, and it's easy to imagine the Indian leader's concern as new farms were built.

In 1675, Philip tried to organize the various regional tribes against the English. He was partially successful, amassing mostly Wampanoag, Nipmuck, and Narragansett warriors, who made scattered raids during that summer. The following year the natives plotted a raid on Medfield.

At the time, Medfield was one of the settlers' outermost towns, with the Charles forming a rough boundary between settlements to the east and wilder country to the west. A prominent Medfield citizen, John Wilson, fearing an attack, wrote Governor Leverett of the Massachusetts Bay Colony: "... Our towne is a frontier town...The losse of Medfeild will be a very greate blow; what will become of the city if the hands of the country grow feeble. Now the rode from Nipmuck is fair for these caniballs, be pleased for God's sake to remember us, and let some considerable sufficient force be sent to us for our speedy releife, before it is too late,...lest Medfeild be turned to ashes..."

A small guard was sent, but the extra men did little to deter the Indian attack on February 21, 1676. Historian William Tilden, author of *The History of the Town of Medfield*, believes the Indians launched their raid from the west side of the Charles River rather than from Noon Hill, where the settlers believed the Indians to be hiding.

The Indian plan was to set every building on fire and then capture or kill the fleeing men, women, and children. Thirty-two homes were burned and seventeen or eighteen people were killed. The death toll could have been much worse, but many whites were able to escape to the town's garrison. The settlers fired their cannons and the Indians "retreated across the bridge over the Charles, setting the bridge on fire at one end to hinder our soldiers from pursuing."

And, so, my peaceful Charles has played a role in warfare. Almost a hundred years later, Paul Revere's ride took him across the mouth of the Charles in the Revolutionary War.

From Route 109, which crosses the Charles, you can walk to historic Medfield Center. Along the way is the Vine Lake Cemetery, where headstones from an earlier age tell a disturbing story of the many people who died before age thirty. One such headstone marks the grave of Sibbel Plymptom, who died in 1753 at twenty-nine. The well-known epitaph speaks a haunting truth:

> *Behold and se You that pafs by*
> *as you be now so once was I*
> *as I am now so you must be*
> *prepare to die and follow me.*

Farther east on Route 109 is a tiny clapboard house with a historical marker labeling it as the Peak House: "The original, built in 1651, was burned when King Philip's Indians burnt the town of Medfield in 1676. Seth Clark, the owner, received indemnity from the colonial government and in 1680 rebuilt the present Peak House, so called because of its architecture."

Medfield also has a number of houses from the 1700s. It seems this area was attractive to settlers because of its many meadows for grazing. As the cattle population grew, more fields were needed, and the woods around the Charles were burned. Today, the woods have grown back, and the river flows through either wetlands or woods, but rarely open fields.

While discussion of the events in the seventeenth and eighteenth centuries may seem like ages ago, it is really recent in terms of the overall history of the Charles. To put recent river history in perspective it's necessary to analyze this region before the glaciers, and few do that better than Henry F. Howe in his book *Salt Rivers of the Massachusetts Shore*. Howe questions whether the Charles was capable of forming the relatively deep, wide channels found in Boston Harbor. He thinks not: "It seems a paradox: here is a great river mouth without a great river." The size of the harbor and river mouth would seem to indicate a river the size of the Hudson or the Connecticut. (It's no wonder Captain John Smith thought the Charles a mighty river whose origin must be far in the interior of the continent.)

Howe offers a plausible explanation for the size of Boston Harbor. There was a huge river here before the glaciers, he reasons, but it was the Merrimack as well as the Charles that spilled into Boston Harbor, where the two rivers merged. When the glaciers came, they blocked the Merrimack's path to Boston, and the river was forced in an easterly direction near Lowell. If you examine a current map of the region and chart the Merrimack's southerly course, it does appear as if it's making a beeline toward Boston. Near Lowell it makes an abrupt turn. It seems the Charles cannot take full credit for forming Boston Harbor.

## Route 109, Millis-Medfield, to Route 27, Sherborn

Route 109 is a popular launching spot for canoeists and I've enjoyed many happy hours paddling through the Great Marsh, consulting my map from time to time. I'm a sucker for any map, but I am especially vulnerable to the green-and-white U.S. Geological Survey maps. The minutes, even the hours, fly by when I pore over these maps, hoping to find some hidden corner of land or perhaps a small island in the Charles that I haven't already discovered. I'm sure I'm not alone in this obsession—lots of outdoorspeople love to search a map for an overlooked trail or a tiny tributary that might hold brook trout. When I look at maps of the Charles, I try to locate a secluded stretch of river with a nice backwater cove. Visions of virgin fishing grounds or undisturbed wildlife are all I need to start scheduling my next trip. Studying these maps in the winter is particularly dangerous and can bring on a terrible case of cabin fever. I own about thirty topo maps, and they inevitably lead to planning a number of excursions, even though I know full well I'll actually only manage to squeeze in a handful. No matter—often, studying the map is as good as being there.

Families often paddle this stretch of the river, and I've seen some of them bring along trash bags to remove any litter they might see along the river. This gives me much-needed optimism after an experience I had nearby. I was fishing under a bridge upstream, when a car went by and tossed a huge bag of trash over the bridge and into the river. The bag just missed me, and although the perpetrator never knew I was standing down there, I immediately dropped my rod and scrambled up the bank in a rage. The car had stopped at an intersection, and I ran up to it, screaming. The driver saw me and took off, probably wondering where this madman in fishing waders had come from. Needless to say, my morning of fishing was ruined.

One can stand on the Route 109 bridge and see for half a mile both upstream and downstream. In the fall it's an especially beautiful view, with fall colors peaking as early as mid-September. The low-lying swamp maples are always the first to turn, and their vivid yellows and reds never disappoint. Farther up the slope of the riverbank, the oaks were showing a touch of brown to offset the dark green of the pines.

Autumn is a good time to canoe this marsh. Because there are no trees, the sun can scorch a canoeist in the summer. Also to be avoided are the strong winds that sometimes kick up; the openness of the marsh makes these winds a real hazard for canoeists. As a young boy, strong winds once pushed my canoe into the shore of a lake, where I had to abandon the vessel and walk three miles through a jungle-like swamp to escape before dark. Also, a friend told me how a strong gust of wind flipped his canoe on Cape Cod's Scargo Lake, spilling him into the icy waters toward the center

*Longtime fishing companion Jon Cogswell, poking around the marsh.*

go Lake, spilling him into the icy waters toward the center of the lake.

This great marsh is part of the Charles River Natural Valley Storage Project of the U.S. Army Corps of Engineers. The project is a recognition that nature often can do a better job than man when it comes to controlling floods. Wetlands play more than a conservation role—they are natural holding areas that act like sponges, allowing the water to spread out rather than race downstream. Perhaps if we now begin to preserve the riverbank, future generations will have at least one green strip left. Gazing into the future can be a bit unsettling—it's a good bet that the entire area from Route 495 east will be developed; protecting the Charles may be our last chance to preserve an oasis of wilderness.

The Massachusetts Rivers Protection Act, signed into law in 1996, accomplishes some of these goals. The act's chief operating mechanism is the establishment of a 200-foot buffer along the river where certain new uses will not be allowed. Existing development and uses are allowed to carry on exactly as they were before the law's enactment. The chief sponsor of the act was Massachusetts state senator Robert Durand (D-Marlborough), who recognized that the riparian buffer established by the bill is a cost-effective means of reducing the impact of polluted runoff into rivers. The buffer strip acts as a natural filter to keep rivers cleaner by absorbing pollution from adjacent development. Bob Zimmerman, executive director of the Charles River Watershed Association, cites the act as a "recognition [that] what happens on land has an impact on water. It's a good thing to have but it's still a status quo bill that won't solve existing problems within the buffer."

Although the act was somewhat watered down during the years of battle it took to turn it into law, it's an important step in the right direction. Once a natural area is developed, it's gone forever, or at least for my lifetime, and canoeing down the Charles past an endless stream of houses and commercial businesses is not my idea of a good time. We are lucky to have a number of reservations along the river, and now with the aid of the Rivers Protection Act we will have saved a few short strips of woods and meadows that surely would have fallen to the ever increasing grind of the bulldozer in our society's quest to develop first and ask questions later. Of course, in my opinion, behind almost every conservation issue looms the bigger problem of rampant population growth...but don't get me started.

Governor William Weld signed the Rivers Protection Act into law on the banks of the Charles at Herder Park in Brighton. He did so in dramatic style, celebrating the com-

*Governor Weld dives into the Charles River after signing the Rivers Protection Bill into law.* Photo by Rose Marston, 1996.

pletion of his signing by diving (fully clothed) into the river with Senator Durand. This demonstrated that the governor:

1) supports the river
2) knows a good photo opportunity
3) knows how to swim.

The marsh supports a wide variety of wildlife and provides an important resting stop for migratory birds that use the Atlantic coastal flyway. During March great flocks of red-winged blackbirds arrive. The males, with their snazzy touch of red, are among the first birds to sing a song of spring. Canada geese also call the marsh home, and some even stay all year. While they look ungainly on the ground (but are still quick enough to shatter a kneecap with their beak if you get too close), once in the air, flying in V-shaped formation, they are a sight to behold. Often, their forlorn honks can be heard long before they can be seen. I recall a time on the river in the fall, when a flock appeared just as the sun was setting. The sun was so low it actually lighted the bellies of the geese, turning them golden against the cold, gray October sky. I was mesmerized. When the birds were out of sight and hearing, the river was strangely still and gentle. Only then did I feel the cold bite in the air, and I began my paddle home.

One animal I have not seen on the river is the eastern coyote, which moved into northern New England from Canada about sixty years ago and is now expanding its range into Massachusetts. I've seen these "little wolves" only in Vermont and in the great tracts of forest abutting the Quabbin Reservoir in central Massachusetts. But there are many coyote living along the Charles, usually leading a nocturnal life.

The few deer that inhabit the Charles River watershed would certainly interest the coyotes. Even though I have seen a number of these deer (including a large buck, seen near Norfolk Center from the window of a commuter train),

I still get a thrill from spotting one. I've had some success using deer calls to bring them in for a close-up camera shot.

I remember an incident that happened when I was using the call (designed to sound like a bleating fawn) from my canoe, anchored near South End Pond in Millis. While I was facing shore to look for any approaching deer, I sent out a series of soft bleats, spaced over ten minutes. Suddenly my hair stood on end as an owl glided by just inches above my head. It had silently approached from the rear, homing in on the sound of the call. I didn't see it until the last minute, and to this day I can still recall the creepy feeling of having become the hunted rather than the hunter. I'm amazed I didn't swamp the canoe in my surprise, and had that owl been a great horned owl, which is truly mammoth, I probably would have had a heart attack.

While I am impressed by the abundance of wildlife in the marsh, I cannot help but wonder what it must have been like even fifty years ago. The best way to find out was to contact my friend Stanley, who explored every inch of the river during the 1930s and 1940s. Stanley Buzarewicz is an anachronism. A trapper by trade, he has never held a "9-to-5" job and has never called any man "boss." Stanley chose to make his living on the land, and often that meant the Charles River marshes. At eighty-two, he still lives in this manner, occasionally trapping, cutting firewood, or "junking"—selling discarded scrap metal found in the woods or along the roadside.

The outdoors shows in his face and his personality. He is a handsome man, tall, with clear blue eyes that literally twinkle when he recalls the Charles of his youth. "You should have seen this place years ago—sights of an incredible abundance of wildlife were commonplace. The muskrat alone seemed to be everywhere. I've seen it out there when the rat [muskrat] houses were so thick you could walk across the marsh on them and never get your feet wet. One day I set forty-five traps, and when I returned I had forty-three rats and the other two traps were missing—maybe otters broke free. There are still a few rats, foxes, and minks around the islands, but nothing like before. They really hurt the wildlife when they started spraying for mosquitoes and doing all the other things they simply don't understand."

Stanley has strong opinions when it comes to what needs to be done to help the river he calls the "mighty Charles": "If we really want to reclaim that river, the bureaucrats need to stop all the rhetoric, and the people need to pass laws that the bureaucrats will enforce. It's the laws rather than departments that will bring the Charles back to the way I knew it."

Stanley is also an amateur archaeologist, with a collection of artifacts that could fill a small museum (he has given away most of them to a variety of historical organizations). I have seen some of his arrowheads, spearheads, ax and tomahawk heads, fishing weights, and even a portion of a stone bowl. One cool November afternoon we took a drive along the upper reaches of the river, where he showed me a place he once found a beautiful quartz point (arrowhead). He explained that the Indians would camp on such spots as this and spear spawning fish, like salmon, as they tried to run the shallow rapids. We searched along the exposed area of the knoll for arrowheads or flakes. The Indians used deer antlers or a piece of stone to make arrowheads by repeatedly striking the rock they were working on until they had chipped away enough flakes to leave a razor-edged, narrow point. Stanley searched the ground for the angular flakes, and after about ten minutes he found one. I could imagine entire Indian families on this hillside, some chipping points in the sun, while others checked their traps and weirs for the day's catch.

We took a walk along the river, and it was obvious that years of outdoor living and labor had served Stanley well. "I never got rich on it, but working in the woods, marshes, and rivers was my sole source of income, and I loved it," he explained. Then he pointed to the road and said, "Just the runoff from the roads, like salt, engine oil, and antifreeze, can really hurt the river."

One of Stanley's favorite places is beautiful South End Pond in Millis. Every winter Stanley is one of the die-hard ice fishermen who fish the pond for yellow perch, crappie, sunfish, pickerel, and largemouth bass. I suspect he comes as much for the camaraderie as for the fish.

South End Pond is fed by the clean waters of Bogastow Brook, which enters from the west, then exits the pond and makes a short run to the Charles. Canoeists on the Charles can easily enter the pond by paddling up Bogastow. Another spot begging exploration is Bridge Island Meadow, an upland meadow and wetland preserved by The Trustees of Reservations and located along the Charles just south of the pond.

Understandably, the Indians favored the South End Pond area—they could camp on the hill above the pond to escape the mosquitoes or use the Charles as their highway either to head inland or go downstream all the way to the bay. Hunting from a dugout canoe surely had its advantages in these meadows, allowing the Indians to glide silently within shooting range of their quarry. How free the Indians must have been hunting and gathering—their work was also their sport.

South End Pond also played a sad role in the history of the local Indian tribes. After King Philip's band of warriors attacked Medfield, they tried to win back South End Pond from the settlers in May 1676. This time the settlers were prepared. Gathered and armed in a garrison of huge stone blocks in Millis, they soundly defeated the charging Indians. The month of May marked the beginning of the end for the Indians who had followed King Philip. Later that year Philip was killed, and the war—along with the Indian way of life on the Charles—was over.

Some of King Philip's followers were hanged and others, including Philip's wife and son, were sold into slavery in the West Indies. The remaining Indians fled to either Canada or New York or submitted to living under the white man's rules on a fraction of their former tribal lands.

From the settlers' viewpoint, the death of King Philip was cause for jubilation. While Boston, just a few miles to the east, was a civilized center of commerce, such towns as Millis were literally the western frontier of eastern Massachusetts, where, during King Philip's uprising, a simple walk to the barn could get you scalped. To place that time period in perspective and to illustrate just how wild the Charles was, consider that the great Lewis and Clark expedition to explore the Great Plains and the Rockies was still 128 years away!

One spring afternoon I canoed the South End Pond area with my wife, Mary Ellen, and Jon and Lisa Cogswell. First we followed Bogastow Brook upstream out of the pond and into the marsh. We were able to land only a few small bass, so we decided to give the pond itself a try. South End Pond is known for its largemouth bass but we got "skunked," yet we still had a wonderful time. Thoreau knew there was more to fishing than catching fish: "His fishing was not a sport, nor solely a means of subsistence, but a sort of solemn sacrament and withdrawal from the world, just as the aged read their Bibles."

For me, fishing is a natural outlet for curiosity: I must discover clues, then play my hunches, which hopefully lead to a successful day of fishing. The fish are the "buried treasure," and long hours of observation are equivalent to the secret map that can lead to its discovery. But unlike a treasure chest, fish are wild creatures and often do the unexpected, which keeps me coming back for more. One such surprise occurred on the Charles when I was angling for bass with a large black rubber worm. I had a hit, successfully worked the fish to shore, and was shocked to see a sixteen-inch rainbow trout at the end of my line. The only explanation for a trout being in that portion of the river is that it must have traveled quite far from its original point of

*Thoreau would appreciate the serenity of this sunny day on the upper Charles.*

stocking that spring. The fact that it was fooled by a rubber worm was even more surprising.

The Cogswells suggested we give the fish a break and head out into the open marshes of the Charles. After we entered the main river, we were content to let the current do the work while we enjoyed the scenery. To our left was a hill covered with an incredible stand of beech trees. This is one of the few places along the river where these magnificent trees can be found, and it is a mystery to me why so many are concentrated in this one spot. In the winter, the beeches are especially attractive because they do not lose all their leaves. Against a backdrop of white snow, the smooth gray trunks and branches with light brown leaves are an impressive sight.

After a short ride downstream, we put out at the Route 27 bridge, also known as Death Bridge, where we had left a second car. Although the name implies a dangerous spot, the truth is innocuous—the bridge was named for the Death family, who lived nearby many years ago. We could see a few cars parked along Route 27. Because we had not seen another vessel on the river all day, we assumed these were the cars of other canoeists who had gone downstream to the popular Rocky Narrows. I guess the upstream stretch of the river was the "road less traveled," and we would not have wanted it any other way.

# Forest Road, Millis, to Route 109, Medfield

## PADDLING

*One Car:* Lots of options—you could launch at Route 109 and paddle upstream or downstream through the huge Millis-Medfield Marsh. Another excellent launch site is on Causeway Street at the Stop River. Heading upstream on this small, winding stream brings you deep into the heart of the Stop River Marsh. Should you choose to follow the current downstream, it's only a short paddle to the confluence with the Charles. From there you paddle upstream, out of the marsh and into the woods near Forest Road.

*Two Cars:* Leave one car at the Route 109 bridge, then drive upstream to Forest Road, where you can launch. The river twists and turns through most of this trip, and travel time may be longer than anticipated. There is a tricky spot at an old bridge abutment at a causeway through the marsh. Be careful. Much of your trip will be through open marsh, so bring supplies (water, extra paddle, life jacket, map, hat, sunscreen, etc.) and avoid windy days or scorching sunny ones. About three or four miles; no portages.

## Route 109, Millis-Medfield, to Route 27, Sherborn

*One Car:* Launch at Route 27 on the border of Sherborn and Medfield and head upstream into the marsh, or put in at South End Pond in Millis and explore it and Bogastow Brook then paddle through the outlet and into the Charles.

*Two Cars:* Leave one car at the Route 27 bridge on the border of Sherborn and Medfield, then drive to the Route 109 bridge on the Millis-Medfield line to launch. The trip is through open marshland, so avoid windy or hot, sunny days and bring supplies. About four miles; no portages, but you may encounter some debris caught in the railroad pilings located about a mile downstream from Route 109. Because of the many curves in the river these trips usually take longer than you might think.

If you think four miles through the marsh might be too monotonous, try launching from South End Pond and have the second car waiting at Route 27. About one and a half miles; no portages.

## RIVER WALKS
*Forest Road, Millis, to Route 109, Medfield*

This area is perhaps the best place on the whole river for hiking, thanks to the two beautiful properties managed by The Trustees of Reservations.

Noon Hill Reservation is between Causeway and Noon Hill Streets in Medfield. It encompasses 204 acres of oak and white pine forest rising above the Charles and Stop Rivers. Noon Hill offers east and southeast views. Early settlers chose the hill's name because the sun lay above the hilltop at noontime as viewed from Medfield Center. Holt Pond is situated on the reservation and looks like the perfect place for a picnic.

The Henry L. Shattuck Reservation lies across the street from Noon Hill, and its 225 acres include 1.25 miles of frontage on the Charles. Every time I visit the reservation, I wish the rest of the Charles were as well protected. You can see wildflowers, deer, fox, ruffed grouse, and many other forms of wildlife.

## Route 109, Millis-Medfield, to
## Route 27, Sherborn

Because of the vast marshland, the river walks are accessible only by canoe. Bridge Island Meadows is a property of The Trustees of Reservations. It features thirty-seven-acre Bridge Island, which lies on the south bank of Bogastow Brook. Good opportunities for viewing wildlife here.

## BIKING

The highlight of this ride is Causeway Street, a country lane that passes by two reservations and the Great Marsh. The total outing is a little more than seven miles on a combination of well-traveled roads and secluded country lanes.

Our trip begins at Causeway Street near its intersection with Forest Road/Orchard Street just east of the bridge that spans the Charles. The beginning of Causeway Street has a few houses, but soon (about half a mile from the start) you pass by the forests of the Shattuck Reservation on the left and Noon Hill Reservation on the right. Shattuck Reservation is reached by the dirt roads that lead from Causeway Street toward the river, and Noon Hill Reservation has an entrance off Noon Hill Road (Noon Hill Road is about 0.8 mile down Causeway Street on the right.) At 1.1 miles down Causeway Street is a dirt road within the Shattuck Reservation that leads to an old bridge abutment along the Charles at the southern end of the Great Marsh. Farther down Causeway Street (1.3 miles from the beginning) you will cross a bridge over the Stop River as you pass by open wetlands and red maple swamps. (Look for wading birds, ducks, and painted turtles along the Stop River.) The final three-fourths of Causeway Street is residential and will bring you to Route 109 about 2.3 miles from the start of your ride.

Turn left on Route 109 and travel 0.3 mile to Bridge Street on your right. Follow Bridge Street 0.8 mile to West Street/Dover Road and go left. You will cross the Charles shortly and there are good views of the marsh to your left. After proceeding a total of 1.2 miles down West Street/Dover Road you will reach Route 109 again, where you should pedal 0.2 mile to the west (a right turn) and look for Village Street on your left. Turn onto Village Street and go 0.8 mile to Forest Road. Turn left on Forest Road, pass gentleman farms, fields, and forest, and proceed about 1.7 miles back to your car by the bridge over the river near Causeway Street.

## BIRDING

Woodland birds, such as ruffed grouse and woodpeckers (including the uncommon pileated woodpecker), are seen upstream from Forest Road where the Charles snakes through quiet forest. The section from the Shattuck Reservation to the Stop River offers good birding as the river passes from thick woodlands to open marsh. (There is a shooting preserve on the west bank of the river just upstream from the Shattuck Reservation, so it's best to do your birding here at dawn when all is quiet.) Great blue herons are abundant here, and I love to see their tracks in the muddy bank, resembling dinosaur footprints. Frequently I see cedar waxwings, warblers, and cardinals near the wooded section and tree swallows in the more open areas.

Another good stretch is the area near the mouth of Bogastow Brook within the Great Marsh. Look for sandpipers, greater and lesser yellowlegs, and killdeer. Friends have seen osprey and an American bittern.

## ANGLING

Good largemouth bass fishing all over the river, including such tributaries as the Stop River, Bogastow Brook, Mill

River, and South End Pond. Carp are scattered throughout the river. Pickerel are in the Great Marsh and South End Pond. Trout are stocked in Millis, Norfolk, and Medfield: try Forest Road in Medfield, Myrtle Street in Norfolk-Millis, River Road in Norfolk, Route 115 in Norfolk-Millis, Mill River on Miller Street in Norfolk, and Bogastow Brook in Millis.

## PICNICKING
The best picnicking is at Noon Hill Reservation in Medfield.

## POINTS OF HISTORIC INTEREST
On Route 109, just east of the center of Medfield, is the Peak House, built just after King Philip's War in 1680. Vine Lake Cemetery on Route 109, just west of the center of Medfield, has tombstones dating back to the 1700s.

# 4

# Rocky Narrows to Old South Natick

I T IS A FINE THING to be on the river during Indian summer. Recently in early November the temperature climbed into the low seventies, and I launched from Route 27 on the Sherborn-Medfield line to paddle through Rocky Narrows, one of the top spots on the river.

With such a name, you would expect this stretch to be a whitewater froth. But the river is actually quite peaceful, and I've noticed only one spot where the river narrows enough to cause a swirl or boil where perhaps the current passes over a granite ledge.

Owned by The Trustees of Reservations, the conservation land, located on the west bank, slopes down to the river, giving the paddler the feeling of being in a tiny canyon. Exposed rock and ledge can be seen in the steepest spots. In three or four places, where the hills meet the river's edge, you can see an impressive stand of eastern hemlock. To me, hemlocks signify the hilly country to the north, and the Charles has very few of these majestic trees—except, of course, those that are found much farther downstream at Hemlock Gorge. Their sweeping branches give the tree a certain gracefulness. Hemlocks are easy to discern from

*A secluded spot near Dover.*

other trees in the pine family because their tops form a dense, pyramid-shaped crown. The chatty red squirrel is a lover of hemlocks, and the Charles has a few of these friendly creatures.

Rocky Narrows is worth exploring by foot. There are a number of places where you can beach your canoe while you hike to the top of a bluff for a better view of the river. (Red-tailed hawks must also like the view, because I often see them here riding thermals above the river.)

I was not alone on the river on such a warm day. A number of families were also enjoying one last outing before winter. I even saw a small boat with an outboard motor heading upstream, but motors of any kind on this part of the Charles are the exception rather than the rule. Outboard motors seem out of place here—the noise alone disrupts the peace and quiet that make the river special and disturbs the many nesting birds and waterfowl. If a motor is necessary, a small electric one would be better suited to the shallow, narrow reaches of the upper Charles.

Only four or five houses can be seen along the stretch from Route 27 to the Farm Road–Bridge Street bridge, and these beautiful homes actually add to the scenery rather than detract from it. One is an incredible estate, sitting high atop a rolling hill, with a swath cleared through the woods to afford the owners an upstream view of the river. The wooden Farm Road–Bridge Street bridge is itself a thing of beauty. This road used to be part of the Old Connecticut Path, a major Indian trail that ran from Massachusetts Bay to the Connecticut River near Hartford. Today, the back roads through this area are secluded as they pass through woods and fields. The launch site at the Farm Road–Bridge Street bridge has room for parking and is considered one of the best on the Charles.

On another trip through Rocky Narrows, I saw a large snapping turtle and then, farther downstream, a reclusive wood duck. The snappers are probably our best example of life from the dinosaur age. While natural extinction overtook most prehistoric species, the snapper adapted. The wood duck, on the other hand, faced extinction from man's hand rather than from any natural occurrence. This colorful little duck was just about wiped out by loss of habitat and overhunting, but is now making a comeback, and this time man is playing a positive role. The wood duck is one of the few birds we can help through building—building nesting boxes, that is, to augment their preferred nests in hollow trees. Whenever I see this crested bird with its splash of green and blue, I feel lucky.

The osprey is another bird that man has tampered with; the pesticide DDT was responsible for reducing its numbers by accumulating in the food chain, causing the osprey's eggshells to grow thin and break under the weight of the nesting parent. Now that DDT has been banned in the U.S. the osprey population is increasing and these birds have been sighted along the Charles. In all my years on the river, I've seen only one osprey, and that was near a small pond in Franklin. Its white belly and the conspicuous crook in its wings made it easy to identify as it circled over the pond in search of fish.

The entire stretch of river from Farm Road to Broadmoor is mostly wooded, with just a few houses in sight. A few hundred feet beyond Farm Road is a sign on the right bank welcoming you to Peters Reservation. I once saw a big buck leave the woods here and cross Glen Street. There are a number of deer in these low-lying woods, and farther downstream, near the remains of an old bridge, I decided to pull over and stretch my legs in hope of seeing one. I hiked back upstream, and although I didn't see any deer, the plantation of red pines was worth the walk. As I got back into my canoe, I heard something move away from the opposite bank—perhaps it was the deer I had been looking for.

As I paddled through the wooded area just beyond Farm Road I savored the last vestiges of fall color. Up ahead,

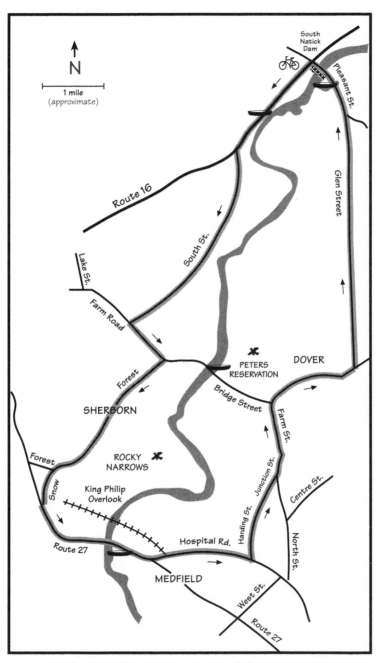

# ROCKY NARROWS–OLD SOUTH NATICK

I got a fleeting glimpse of an otter before it disappeared beneath the riverbank. Otters can swim underwater for almost half a mile. They make their homes in burrows on the riverbank or under a maze of tree roots by the water's edge, and in their playful moods they often slide down the riverbank on snow or mud. There are no better fishermen than otters. They hunt down just about every species of fish and supplement their diet with snails, frogs, crayfish, and even a bird if it happens to fall into the river. I recall ice fishing at South End Pond with Stanley last winter and discovering a muskrat house that had been taken over by an otter. There was a large hole in the top of the stick-and-mud house where the otter had either entered or exited. Stanley knew it was an otter, because on the side of the house was a pile of fish scales, which Stanley said were from otter droppings (muskrat don't eat fish). Walking near the river with Stanley is the next best thing to walking with a hunter from the Massachusetts tribe of Indians who roamed these parts more than three hundred years ago.

While otters are somewhat rare on the Charles, muskrat are not, although Stanley tells me they are nowhere near as numerous as they once were. There must have been "rats" everywhere during Stanley's younger days, because I often see them on the river now; in fact, I've even seen them searching through grassy banks during the early spring. The muskrat I remember best was the one that almost caused me to take a spill in the icy waters of the Charles last spring. I was fishing in hip boots at dawn when a muskrat swam toward me; either it didn't see me, or perhaps it was merely curious. In the gray light, I didn't notice the muskrat until it was five inches from my thigh. Now, I know it doesn't sound macho to say I was scared by a muskrat, but believe me, I was startled when I looked down toward the water and saw something looking back at me.

The muskrat is a food source for minks, hawks, foxes, owls, and even large snappers. Fortunately, the muskrat is

*Ice formation from receding water on Farm Road bridge in Dover.*

so prolific that its population remains stable despite its high mortality rate. The Indians, ever resourceful, used the muskrat for more than just its meat and pelt. Both muskrat and Indians were fond of the sweet roots of the yellow pond lily. The Indians would let the muskrat gather and then cache the roots. In the fall, the Indians would raid the storehouses and help themselves to the roots. Howard Russell, in his fascinating book *Indian New England before the Mayflower,* describes how the Indians were careful to leave the muskrat enough food to survive the winter. Again, we see the Indians' understanding of interdependence and their concept of the "whole": the muskrat had a place on the river; each plant and animal made up an integral part of the whole of life.

Floating along, I gazed into the thick woods and thought how different these woods in the Sherborn-Dover area might have looked in the days of the Indian. Certainly the trees would have been bigger; the forests we now see are second or third growth. Incredibly, there are no large tracks of virgin forests left in the state. The accounts of early explorers indicate that the woods were open enough to march an army through. The forests resembled parkland, with tall trees growing several feet apart, because the Indians would burn off the low growth each year to make hunting easier.

I can imagine young Indian children running through the forest. Day after day, these youngsters learned the ways of the forest and river while enjoying childhood to its fullest. This freedom did not go unnoticed by the Puritan settlers, and there are accounts of settlers' complaints that the Indian children were undisciplined.

When I see families enjoying a day on the river, the children never look bored. There are plenty of unusual plants and wildlife to arouse a child's curiosity. Around Boston, the Charles is just about the only natural area with miles of public access. On nearby lakes, houses cover almost every inch of the shoreline, and it's virtually impossible for a child to get out of the boat to take a closer look at some shoreline plant or bird.

One place where you might spot an interesting bird like an osprey or wood duck is the sprawling Broadmoor Wildlife Sanctuary on the banks of the Charles in Natick. The Audubon Society assembled this preserve through gifts and purchases beginning in 1962. Today Broadmoor is a much-needed sanctuary in the midst of suburbia.

When I lived in Natick, I would often hike through Broadmoor's many trails, observing painted turtles, kingfishers, kestrels, grouse, woodchucks, and many other occupants of the sanctuary. The Mill Pond–Marsh Trail was always a treat, with delicate pink lady-slippers blooming in spring and pond lilies growing in the water during the summer. The trail brings you to the stone foundations of Thomas Sawin's gristmill, built in the late 1600s. Sawin eventually sold his mill due to the constant pressure of angry upstream residents who claimed his dam was responsible for backing up the flow of the Charles, flooding their fields. However, new owners of the dam simply continued its operation.

The Charles River Trail that runs along the river can be reached by going down the Mill Pond–Marsh Trail and crossing South Street. A diverse variety of birds can be seen here, including blue-winged teal, ring-necked ducks, yellow-bellied cuckoos, tree swallows, great crested flycatchers, and red-eyed vireos, to name just a few.

The history of Broadmoor is as diverse and interesting as its birdlife. Of course, the region was first inhabited by the native American Indians, primarily the Massachusetts tribe. The plague of 1616–17, which may have been a result of diseases contracted from the first European settlers, decimated all the eastern tribes, including those living in the Natick area. In 1650, a new band of Indians, led by John Eliot, settled in the area that is now part of Broadmoor. As we shall see later, these Indians had adopted some of the white man's ways and for years brought their grain to Medfield and

Watertown to be ground. They decided they needed a gristmill closer to home, and Thomas Sawin, a Sherborn carpenter, was allowed by the Indians to construct a mill near the confluence of the Charles and Indian Brook in 1692. The mill was operational under various owners until 1918, by which time the Indians had long since sold or been cheated out of their land.

Continuing down the Charles, just a little way past Broadmoor, is the mysterious "praying woman" statue, standing on a boulder by the side of the river. All sorts of myths have surrounded the statue, the most common being that it was erected in memory of a child who drowned in the river. But while I was doing research at Natick's Morse Institute Library, librarian/historian Carol Coverly let me in on the secret. She produced a typewritten copy of an interview she conducted a few years ago with the late Daniel Sargent, a writer who had lived on a small estate beside the Charles in South Natick. While interviewing Sargent about the history of South Natick, Carol happened to ask if he knew anything about the statue on the Charles River. Sargent answered, "You mean *my* statue?" Carol, taken aback, asked, "That is *your* statue? A lot of people ask us about it." Sargent explained that the statue is of Our Lady. He went on, "People have a tendency to tell these stories about the statue. All sorts! One lady said to another, 'Do you know about that statue?' 'Yes, it is modeled after a mistress he had in Paris!' It wasn't true!"

The statue was the idea of Sargent's wife, and he thought the large rock above the river would be the perfect place for it. This was just before the Depression, and Sargent reflected: "I did it when I had the money. If I had waited, I probably would never have done it." I'm certainly glad he did. The statue adds a touch of enchantment to the river, and even though it surprises the passing canoeist, it somehow seems to fit the riverbank's landscape perfectly.

*The mysterious praying woman statue.*

Sargent also had an ornate wooden footbridge erected over the river. You can launch your canoe from the park near the South Natick Dam and paddle upstream to view the bridge and the statue or, if you have two cars, put in at the Farm Road bridge and let the current bring you past them and, eventually, to the second car at South Natick.

Below Sargent's bridge, the river widens as it moves toward the South Natick Dam. When my wife and I were dating during the early 1980s, we canoed this area frequently. I had the brains not to bring a fishing rod during our courtship; if she had any idea of my passion for fishing, she probably never would have married me.

There are many places on the river that bring back memories of special events or special friends. I'm sure I'm not the only person who has personalized different spots with homemade names like "Dale's Run." The only people who know where Dale's Run is are Dale, myself, and a couple of other anglers—we all know it's where Dale caught his six-pound largemouth bass.

My most memorable South Natick fish was a medium-sized largemouth. He was no monster; it's the way he hit that I'll remember. I was absent-mindedly pitching a top-water plug (I believe it was a Heddon Tiny Torpedo) during an afternoon when the fish simply were not feeding. I had reeled the plug all the way back to the canoe, when the bass slammed it and woke me up in a hurry. He was so close to the canoe, all I had to do was scoop him up in the net. For heart-thumping action, nothing beats a surface strike.

The small park around the South Natick Dam is an inviting gathering spot in the summer, with picnic tables and benches set beneath the trees. In the springtime, anglers can fish for stocked trout in the oxygenated quick water beneath the falls. The dam itself is a thing of beauty, as is the stone bridge. As beautiful as this spot is, however, I wish there were no dams on the river, because they alter the river's

*Sargent's Bridge, an ornate wooden footbridge, spanning the Charles in Natick.*

natural flow, increasing stagnation and raising water temperature.

There are now twenty dams on the Charles, and just about every one was a source of controversy when it was built. Each time a dam was erected for power, someone downstream felt the effects it had on water volume. Upstream residents complained of the water backing up, submerging their low-lying fields. In the late 1600s, anyone who owned land abutting both sides of the river could erect a dam to form a millpond and guarantee a steady source of water. The disputes became something akin to those of the Hatfields and McCoys, with threats, illegal blocking of the river's flow, and a steady stream of court action in the form of suits, countersuits, and appeals. As more dams were built, the fishermen joined the battle when they realized anadromous fish (which return from the sea to spawn in the river), could no longer make it up the river.

The first dams were built either to grind corn or saw timber. The mill wheels turned via the water power that flowed from the millpond through a millrace and then over or under the wheel, depending on the type of construction. The mill owners had a good business arrangement: local residents needed their corn milled or their timber sawn, and the mill owners had free use of the Charles to do the job. And while the customers waited for their corn to be ground or logs to be cut, they could shop or perhaps have a drink at the adjacent store or inn, which usually were owned by the mill owner.

In the early 1800s, the mills were expanded for such industries as ironworks and paper and textile manufacturing. On the sites of the old mills, with their two or three employees, were now factories employing hundreds. More dams were needed, causing even more confrontations over the flow of the Charles. In a Charles River Watershed Association booklet, "Charles River Dams," historian Thelma Fleishman explains that there was not enough water power

*The beautiful Old South Natick dam.*

to operate all three of the mills in Medway at the same time. The solution to the problem was simple: "The same group of workers moved from mill to mill, from the uppermost where enough water for about four hours of work collected in the pond overnight, down to the next where the wastewater from above was impounded for another four hours, and so on to the third."

The mills took their toll on the Charles by discharging such pollutants as the dyes released at textile mills, and stagnating the water behind the dams. It was even alleged that the variation in water flow caused malaria by exposing vast mud flats and areas of vegetation that would normally be submerged. Our generation compounded the problems by locating town dumps near the river in places too wet for building.

I'm sure ocean-dwelling fish that used the Charles for spawning were not the only species to be hurt by the dams. Native brook trout, which require clean, oxygenated water, probably suffered as well. Unfortunately the dams, which have outlived their original purpose, will remain because the land along the river is too developed to allow for their removal.

Millis and Medfield are not the only towns whose beginnings were shaped by contact with the American Indian. However, unlike the Indian skirmishes in Millis and Medfield, South Natick's history involves peaceful Indians under the guidance of John Eliot.

John Eliot was a Puritan minister and missionary, respected by a great many whites and Indians because he was a sincere man. He recognized the dangers of the friction between the settlers and Indians and thought the best way to help the Indians was to convert them to the white man's ways and religion. His first Indian followers were from the towns immediately surrounding Boston, including Newton, where the Nonantum band lived. As word of John Eliot's work spread among the Indians, some from as far away as

Concord joined his following, first established in the Newton area.

Eliot's goal was to find a large tract of land where these Christian Indians could begin a community modeled after the English. After a long search, he secured 2,000 acres farther up the Charles. In 1650, Eliot and his Indians canoed upstream to their new home at South Natick.

The settlement was on both sides of the Charles, and immediately the Indians began construction of an eighty-foot wooden bridge across the river. They built a large meetinghouse and cleared land on the south side of the river for cornfields. The experiment had mixed results: While the Indians were known as the "praying Indians" and there were some English-style buildings erected on the north side of the river, language, customs, and cultural differences were so deep that the Indians never totally adapted to the settlers' way of life.

One reason the experiment failed was the treatment these Christian Indians received during King Philip's War. Even though the Natick Indians were peaceful during the conflict, the fearful settlers restricted them to the Indian settlement or, in some cases, imprisoned them. Most of the imprisoned Indians were placed on Deer Island in Boston Harbor, while others were incarcerated on an adjacent island. It is estimated that 500 Indian men, women, and children endured disease and hunger for two years on these islands. Some Indians were released early, when the colonists, who had suffered great losses during the first few months of King Philip's War, turned to the very Indians they had imprisoned to assist them in their struggle. Some of the male Christian Indians were organized to act as spies. Later, they were armed to fight against King Philip, and it is said that their knowledge of the enemy and the terrain helped turn the tide of the war.

The Christian Indian community continued for more than a century before finally failing, when the impoverished

Indians were forced to sell their lands. The lesson from this experiment seems clear—one society simply cannot force its culture on another.

By the 1800s, Natick had evolved into a major shoe-manufacturing town. It was equally well known as the setting for Harriet Beecher Stowe's novel *Old Town Folks*. The Harriet Beecher Stowe House on Pleasant Street, within sight of the South Natick Dam, was the boyhood home of the author's husband, Calvin Stowe (Horace Holyoke of the novel). After she had written *Uncle Tom's Cabin*, Mrs. Stowe began *Old Town Folks*, completed in 1869. The novel, which many readers felt was her best, is based upon her husband's recollections of growing up along the banks of the Charles in the little village of South Natick. The opening pages of *Old Town Folks* describe South Natick and the Charles: "It was as pretty a village as ever laid down to rest on the banks of a tranquil river. The stream was one of those limpid children of the mountains whose brown, clear waters ripple with a soft yellow light..."

South Natick is still a beautiful place. The Harriet Beecher Stowe House is part of the John Eliot Historical District, which includes a number of historic homes, a small museum, the Eliot Church, and the Indian Burial Grounds. The focal point of the area is still the Charles, however, just as it was when John Eliot and his Indians arrived in 1650.

The present South Natick Dam was built in the 1930s to replace a wooden dam damaged by the great flood of 1885. Old photographs taken during the flood can be seen at Natick's Morse Institute Library. These show a devastated area, with townsmen in their overcoats using boats to pass flooded streets. The 1935 dam was made of concrete, and the fish ladder was one of the first ones built, after almost total neglect in the 1800s of the needs of migrating fish. Even this ladder doesn't look like too many fish could actually climb it, and it is scheduled to be rebuilt when the state budget allows.

*An enjoyable quiet-afternoon spot.*

While I was looking at the old photos, Carol Coverly showed me a manuscript written fifty years ago by Florence Lovell Macowen, who lived from 1861 to 1948. Apparently the manuscript lay hidden in the vault of a Natick bank for many years. The handwritten notes eventually found their way to the Natick Historical Commission and, with Carol Coverly's help, were typed into a complete manuscript. Author Macowen loved the Charles and devoted one whole chapter to describing its beauty. She accurately depicts the essence of the river's flow when she writes: "It is not a noisy, rushing stream, but has many windings through hills, valleys, and towns…"

In Macowen's time, the river was a more popular recreation spot than it is today, with picnicking, rowing, and swimming along the Natick stretch of the Charles. Reading her account of the Charles made me realize what a historic treasure the river is. And even today, except for certain spots, such as Norumbega and the Charles River Basin, one can canoe the river and never see another soul.

# Recreation Guide

## Rocky Narrows to Old South Natick

### PADDLING

*One Car:* Try launching from the Farm Road–Bridge Street bridge on the Dover-Sherborn line. Head upstream through a small marshy area and into Rocky Narrows. Or launch at the little park above the South Natick Dam and go upstream roughly one mile to view the enchanting footbridge and statue. There is also a small launch site next to Route 16, about 200 yards upstream of the statue.

*Sarah and Mamie Andrews canoeing circa 1884, when the Upper Charles was a more popular recreation spot.* Photo courtesy of the Charles River Watershed Association.

*Two Cars:* For perhaps the best ride on the river in terms of natural scenery, leave one car at the South Natick Dam and then drive upstream to launch at the Route 27 bridge on the Sherborn-Medfield line. This ride takes you through the bluffs of Rocky Narrows, under the old Farm Road–Bridge Street bridge, through acres of forest, past Broadmoor Wildlife Sanctuary, past the praying woman statue, under the footbridge, and then into the broad waters above the South Natick Dam. Takeout should be on the right bank above the dam at the small town park. About five miles; no portages.

## RIVER WALKS
### *Rocky Narrows to Old South Natick*

The 150 acres of Rocky Narrows is accessible by canoe, or from Route 27 by foot. The canoe landing is on the west (Sherborn) side of the river. The granite ledges, towering hemlocks, and good opportunities for seeing wildlife make this a special place. The colonists regarded this area as "the Gates of the Charles" and built a fort here for protection against the Indians. The Rocky Narrows Reservation is located on the west bank of the Charles.

Broadmoor Wildlife Sanctuary provides some of the best nature trails on the river. Located off Route 16 in Natick, the sanctuary has a diversity of terrain and excellent birding—bring your binoculars. This sanctuary, run by the Audubon Society, is a great place to bring the kids.

Peters Reservation in Dover is a recent addition to the Charles River Protection Program. The property was donated by bequest of Jane Peters Guild in 1988 and is now managed by The Trustees of Reservations. The property features 2,047 feet of frontage along the Charles. Enter from Bridge Street in Dover.

# BIKING

This chapter and the next feature my favorite bicycle rides along the Charles, which are also two of the best outings found anywhere in eastern Massachusetts. Gentle, rolling terrain coupled with quiet back roads passing by woods and gentleman farms make for a winning combination with frequent views of the Charles. Historic sites abound, as do many quiet places that are perfect for picnics. This is a long ride (thirteen miles), so bring water and don't forget your camera!

Our ride begins at the South Natick Dam, where there is plenty of parking on the Mill Street cutoff next to the dam or on the shoulder of Pleasant Street. Follow Route 16 westward—this is an upstream direction in relation to the Charles—and proceed with caution as this is one of the few roads on our ride that can be busy during rush hours. At the half-mile mark you will be able to look out across the river and see the praying woman statue, and by turning to look downstream a short distance you can see the private footbridge that spans the Charles.

When you have gone one mile turn left on South Street. (If you were to continue straight on Route 16 for another half-mile you would reach the entrance to Broadmoor Wildlife Sanctuary.) South Street is a less-traveled, narrow back road that passes through the forests of Broadmoor Wildlife Sanctuary and over a small brook with a handsome stone bridge (best seen from stream level). Farther down the road you pedal by fields where deer and hawks are sometimes seen. The last section of South Street is perhaps the most scenic because the road is lined by large white pines (providing almost total shade for bicyclists on hot summer days).

After traveling a total of 1.8 miles on South Street, turn left onto Farm Road. As you cruise downhill on Farm Road the view is fantastic with rolling fields and barns painted red and white. Be sure to explore the old graveyard tucked beneath the hemlock trees on your left just before you reach Forest Road on your right at 0.8 mile.

Our ride goes right on Forest Road but you might first want to continue down Farm Road a short distance to the bridge that spans the Charles. This is a popular launching spot and the bridge provides scenic vistas of both the river and paddlers. (If you are feeling tired and want to shorten the ride you can simply cross the bridge and turn left, following the directions on the map to return to the South Natick Dam via Glen Street. From the Farm Road bridge it is only 3.5 miles to the dam.)

Our ride continues by following Forest Road to the southwest as it hugs a wooded ridge where coyotes are sometimes seen crossing the road. About a mile ahead is a parking lot for Rocky Narrows Reservation on the left. The network of trails from this particular entrance to the reservation are confusing, but for bicyclists the broad meadow near the road makes a fine place to stop, rest, and catch a few rays. (Another land access to the reservation is still ahead on Route 27.) Continue bicycling on Forest Road until you see a sign for Snow Street at a fork in the road about 1.6 miles from when you first entered Forest Road. Bear left on Snow Street and follow it 0.3 mile to its intersection with Route 27, where you should turn left.

About 0.2 mile down Route 27 you will see another parking lot for Rocky Narrows, where a trail system leads to the King Philip Overlook. Next, Route 27 crosses the Charles at the old Death Bridge site. After pedaling for a total of 1.2 miles down Route 27, turn left onto Hospital Road. Follow Hospital Road for 1.1 miles past open fields to Harding Street, where you should turn left. Harding Street is a residential road that leads into Farm Street after 1.1 miles. Turn left on Farm Street and proceed 1.4 miles, passing handsome estates, stone walls, and meadows. Glen Street will be on your left; turn here and bicycle down this straight road 2.4 miles to its end. (Be on the lookout for the entrance to Saint Stephen Priory at 0.3 mile on Glen Street—the entrance road is perfectly lined by tall trees, making for a visual treat, especially in the autumn.) When you reach the end of Glen Street turn left on Pleasant Street, and in 0.2 mile you will be back at your car. There are plenty of benches and picnic tables at which to rest and enjoy the waterfall at the dam.

## BIRDING

The entire run from Rocky Narrows to the South Natick Dam is excellent bird habitat, with many reservations lining the Charles to keep the riparian corridor in its natural state. Look for such wading birds as great blue herons and green-backed herons in the setbacks. I've seen Eastern kingbirds perched on branches above the river, calmly surveying the Charles, and farther downstream by Broadmoor Wildlife Sanctuary there is good viewing for owls. Look up into the pine trees and you may see a great horned owl quietly passing the day as it waits for dusk to fall to begin hunting. (Owls are one of the few predators that feed on skunks. A friend reported seeing an owl near the river perched in a tree with a dead skunk in its talons.)

Some of the birds seen along the river by visitors to Broadmoor Wildlife Sanctuary include northern oriole, belted kingfisher, eastern phoebe, common yellowthroat, green-backed heron, and northern flicker. Dozens more birds have been recorded, but one of my favorites is the northern goshawk, a grayish brown raptor that will attack anyone who comes near its nest!

## ANGLING

Largemouth bass and carp all over the river, and pickerel in the setbacks. Trout at the South Natick Dam.

## PICNICKING

King Philip Overlook and Rocky Narrows offer picnicking with a view. The canoe landing at Rocky Narrows offers riverside picnicking as does the open space around the South Natick Dam and the Elm Falls/Cochrane Dam area. Farther from the Charles there is picnicking at Oak Grove Farm on Route 115 in Millis and Noanet Woodlands on Dedham Road in Dover.

## POINTS OF HISTORIC INTEREST

The historic village of South Natick is worth exploring by foot (see text concerning the Harriet Beecher Stowe House, praying Indian community, and history of South Natick). The Bacon Free Library next to the South Natick Dam is a wonderful place to visit, and has a fascinating museum in the basement. The bridge at the South Natick Dam is a handsome stone structure built in 1857. Broadmoor Wildlife Sanctuary has evidence of an old mill site, including the millstone.

On Farm Road in Sherborn about a half-mile from the river, a tiny old cemetery can be found nestled beneath the pines and hemlocks. Interesting headstone inscriptions.

## CANOE RENTAL

Tropicland Marine & Tackle
100 Bridge Street, Dedham
617-329-3777

Directions: From Route 128 take Route 109 east into Dedham; Tropicland will be on the right side of the road.

# 5

## South Natick to Dedham

**M**AY IS A DIFFICULT month for outdoorspeople. All of nature comes alive, and so many outdoor activities are available it is hard to pursue them all. My garden beckons, but so does the river; freshly stocked trout, awakening bass, the stirrings of wildlife, and the return of migratory birds put the Charles at the top of my list. Although I walk along the banks of the river throughout the winter, seeing the Charles in all its spring glory is like visiting an old friend.

The river has surprises around each bend—some good, some bad, and some that simply confuse. Confusion is just what the Charles occasionally produces below the South Natick Dam. The river here is similar to the upstream stretch, except for one feature: it has numerous coves and setbacks that have left me temporarily lost more than once.

These coves are worth the trouble, however. The pickerel and bass fishing can be tremendous. The rather ugly, prehistoric-looking pickerel just love the weedy setbacks, and even when the bass are in their midday doldrums, pickerel will still cooperate—especially when the lure or plug is red. Like an enraged bull, a pickerel will charge a flash of crimson.

*A young angler crosses the river below the South Natick dam.*

I was fishing with Jon Cogswell when a huge pickerel slammed my lure on the first twitch. Long before I had netted the brute I was "counting my chickens" with a bit of boasting directed toward Cogs. I figured my twelve-pound-test line was heavy enough to land a bluefish, and I anticipated no problems with a pickerel. Not so. The fish made one roll on the surface and the line snapped, perhaps severed by its long row of teeth. My cursing gave way to muttering, followed by some big-time pouting. Cogs sat silently through both the tirade and my subsequent brooding. I knew he would not forget the incident, though, and would wait for the most opportune time to call attention to my behavior. Most likely he would wait a few months, and then at some get-together would say casually, "Mike, tell everyone about the giant pickerel you played so well that day on the Charles."

The good fishing we enjoy on the Charles remains something of a secret, even to residents of eastern Massachusetts. Perhaps the river is underutilized by anglers because many of the best spots require some searching, far from the nearest launch site. The late Dick Cronin, who was director of the Massachusetts Division of Fisheries and Wildlife, referred to the Charles as a "sleeping giant," which was his way of saying that the river's vast recreational potential, particularly fishing, had not yet been tapped.

The Charles isn't the only river bypassed by anglers who prefer the convenience of lakes. John Madson, in *Up On the River: An Upper Mississippi Chronicle* (truly one of the great river books), detailed the high-quality largemouth fishery that goes overlooked on the Mississippi. Madson adds: "Still, for one reason or another, the bass appear to be one of the better-kept secrets in the Upper Mississippi sport fishery."

One angler I know has had great fishing in the late spring, when some of the river's backwaters recede, sealing the entrance to the main river. The fish get trapped inside, and before long the largemouths are ravenous, willing to strike just about anything an angler tosses in.

About three-quarters of a mile below the South Natick Dam lies the Elm Bank Reservation on the south bank. This is a good spot to stretch your legs with a walk through the fields. There is also a riverside trail that offers superb hiking. Green-backed herons and black-crowned night herons are sometimes seen wading along the shore at Elm Bank.

Another three-quarters of a mile farther downstream lies the mouth of Waban and Fuller Brooks on the left. I'm told that it's possible to work a canoe up Waban Brook to Lake Waban, but I've never made this run, preferring instead to launch my canoe directly into the lake, which is situated on the beautiful grounds of Wellesley College.

On a recent walk through this area, it was easy to spot the real harbinger of spring—the skunk cabbage, with its unpleasant smell. With the first hint of warm weather, the skunk cabbage pokes itself through the swamp floor and begins to uncurl the dark green-and-purple leaves that release the skunky scent. It's usually the first bit of green I see in the woods, and I actually welcome its odor as a sign of the warm days to come. When the skunk cabbage sprouts, flocks of male red-winged blackbirds cannot be far behind. The females arrive a week or two later, and the marshes along Lake Waban and the Charles are alive with swooping birds keeping up a constant chatter.

Back on the river, the coves become larger and more numerous, forming a number of small peninsulas where the water curls backward in an upstream direction. This area is perfect for the explorer in all of us; many of the setbacks have a number of little spikes or fingers to investigate, while others, such as the one between Trout Brook and Centre Street on the Dover-Needham town line, are big enough to be called ponds. Trout Brook itself forms a large cove where it enters the Charles, and the view of this area from Clay-brook Street is quite inviting—yet another backwater slough on the Charles for future exploration.

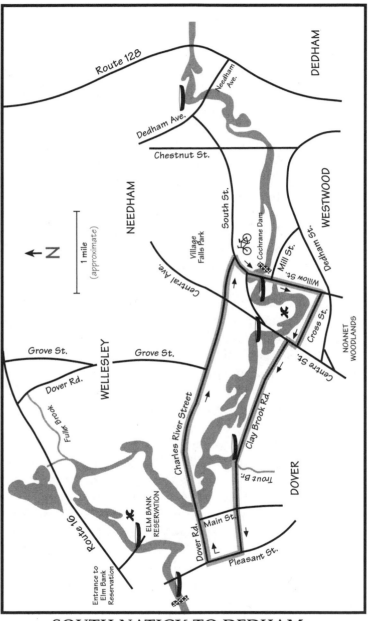

**SOUTH NATICK TO DEDHAM**

Claybrook and Mill Streets (farther downstream) are back roads that follow the river, with some portions running right along the water. These country lanes are great for bicycling—I can view both the river and some fine old New England houses at the same time. The recent creation of bike paths along the lower portion of the river is the only development on the Charles I favor.

This bucolic stretch of the Charles has always reminded me of Claude Monet's *Branch of the Seine*. The painting is done in shades of blue, purple, and green, depicting large, leafy trees overhanging the smooth, flowing river. I bought a print of this painting and hung it in my office because the peaceful scene transports me to the Charles whenever I look at it.

Peacefulness is what the Charles is all about: with few rapids, this slow-flowing river's natural state is quiet and calm, like a friend who never gets flustered. The river takes its time on the way to the bay—poking along, going north then south, east then west, as if to say, "What's the rush?"

And the quiet friend can also be a bit mysterious, especially on fall mornings when mist hugs the marshes. A thick mist always has a calming effect on me, and those early morning paddles are priceless. When the gray, hazy fog obscures the shoreline, it's as if the river, the canoe, and I are the only things on earth. This feeling is reinforced by the insulating effects of the fog—outside sounds are muffled, but the strokes of my paddle seem loud.

While morning is my favorite time on the river, evening is a close second. Sure, mosquitoes are out, launching sorties on the unprotected, but a little insect repellent usually does the trick. I often go down to the river after work to get in a couple of hours of fishing before dark. The best time is just before complete darkness falls, when the granddaddy largemouths begin their nocturnal prowling. Nighttime smells alone are worth the trip. The cool smells of earth, water, and organic matter can be detected only after the sun sets. An occasional splash in the river or the hoot of an owl only serve

*These cheerful river inhabitants greet anglers and canoeists loudly.*

to enhance the mood of tranquillity. However, after working at a frenzied pace all day in the city, it does take me a few minutes to fully appreciate the river's mood. When my senses adjust to the magic of twilight, it's easy to sit back and soak in the solitude. Whether night or day, the Charles provides me with a slice of wilderness in suburbia.

     The twenty-nine-acre Charles River Peninsula is located on the north side of the river off Fisher Street in Needham.

The rolling fields that lead down to the Charles are great for strolling (but watch out for the groundhog holes). One morning in November I walked the perimeter of the fields, peering into the pockets of brush in search of wildlife. A red-tailed hawk screeched its displeasure over my intrusion as it glided away. I was not surprised that a hawk would call this area home, since there were tracks of small game crisscrossing the tall field grass. When I hike here I rarely see any other people.

On another walk through the peninsula, I saw one of New England's most unique creatures—the opossum. The opossum is a nocturnal animal, and this was the first one I had seen in the wild. For years I had seen them dead on the road, and I always wondered where they hid themselves during the daytime. This one was foraging about at the edge of the field near the railroad tracks. With his pointed snout and long tail, he was definitely odd looking. Rather than "playing possum" when I approached, he simply scurried into dense cover, and I had no time to focus my telephoto lens. The opossum is related to the kangaroo and is the only marsupial native to North America. Hunting opossum is common in the South, and baked opossum is considered a delicacy in some places. I'm sure the Indians ate them, as well as just about every other creature indigenous to the region, such as snapping turtles. Perhaps the Indians would find our tendency to eat only beef, pork, and chicken boring and bland.

For those hikers looking for an even larger area, try nearby Noanet Woodlands, located off Dedham Street in Dover. Like so many other scenic and ecologically important properties in the state, Noanet is owned and operated by The Trustees of Reservations. The 591-acre property offers hiking, jogging, cross-country skiing, picnicking, and fishing in Noanet Brook, which is just one of the many feeder streams to the Charles. The brook powered the Dover Union Iron Company in the 1800s, and you can hike to the old mill site by taking the Peabody

*A quiet launch site at the heavily wooded Elm Bank Reservation
(Wellesley-Dover).*

Trail. Another trail worth taking is the one that leads to 387-foot Noanet Peak, which offers a view of the Boston skyline.

Just below the Charles River Peninsula is an area of the river known as Redwing Bay, which features a boat launch on Fisher Street constructed by the Metropolitan District Commission (MDC). The MDC has been instrumental in preserving land along the lower half of the Charles and also in providing recreational access and opportunities on the river. Much of its current effort involves working with communities to create buffer zones along the Charles and to ensure that any future development on the river does not have an adverse impact on water quality. The MDC has jurisdiction from the mouth of the Charles all the way to the South Natick Dam. Upstream from South Natick, the task of protecting the river falls to individual communities. The Charles River Watershed Association is the only organization I know of that is trying to protect the upper Charles. Concerned citizens need to support the association and develop a strong, coordinated approach for preserving the remaining natural areas along the river.

The next interesting feature on the Charles lies just below Redwing Bay, where the Cochrane Dam spans the river at the junction of Mill and Willow Streets in Dover. The fast water below the dam is a popular spot for kayakers. Extended across the river are a few ropes, from which hang long wooden poles that act as gates for the kayakers to maneuver through. Those who come here to test their skill range from the recreational kayaker seeking a workout to experts hoping for a spot in the Olympics.

On a Sunday morning one December, I visited this area and, despite the cold weather, found three kayakers (wearing wet suits) enjoying the perfect conditions caused by recent rains. One fellow told me that during the summer they had trouble with kids who pulled down the gates while swimming. I was somewhat amazed that anyone would attempt to swim in these waters. It is not pollution that concerns me, but rather the river's naturally murky waters. A swimmer simply cannot see what is beneath him, and the Charles has many submerged obstructions. Perhaps someday the river will once again have designated swimming areas, but until such time, it's a dangerous activity.

Watching the kayakers was quite humbling; it must take enormous upper-body strength to paddle against a strong current, then briefly hold the vessel steady while positioning it for a dash through the gate. Their power must be matched by perfect timing. The cold seemed to have no effect on the kayakers—the proper water level and flow was their only concern. It looked like a sport I'd love to try, but the last thing I need is another hobby.

While watching the kayakers shoot the rapids, I began to wonder about the fishing here. Although largemouths would find this water a bit too rough, it seemed like a great place to stock smallmouth bass. Unlike their bucket-mouthed cousins, the feisty bronze-backed smallmouth prefers a boulder-strewn stretch of quick water over slow, lazy water. Smallmouths have done quite well in a number of New England rivers, such as the Housatonic in Connecticut, the Deerfield in Massachusetts, the Saco in Maine, the Merrimack in New Hampshire, the White River in Vermont, and just about the entire length of the Connecticut River. I'll have to contact the Massachusetts Division of Fisheries and Wildlife to see if smallmouths would be feasible in the Charles; pound for pound nothing I know of can outfight a smallie. Their surface-to-air leaps are more spectacular than those of rainbow trout, and God only knows how many bronzebacks I've lost when they combine a jump with a twist and shake a plug free.

The area near Cochrane Dam is called the Charles River Village, which, like so many other spots along the river, was a mill village in an earlier age. Over a 250-year period, the mills here produced a wide range of products including nails, iron, rubber, paper, and cloth. It must have been a bustling area then; today it's a quiet mix of residences and woods.

While the area below the Cochrane Dam is great for experienced kayakers, I think most canoeists are wise to avoid the entire stretch all the way to Needham Avenue. Besides the minifalls created by an MDC sewer conduit that crosses the river, there are quite a few boulders, shallow spots, and a tricky drop-off upstream from Needham Avenue. For those experienced paddlers who don't mind a few obstructions, the area is canoeable and offers considerable beauty in the form of fields, woodlands, and well-kept homes and estates.

Perhaps a better place to launch is on South Street, near where Needham Avenue crosses the Charles. If you do start your excursion from here, you will immediately see a large rocky ledge sloping into the river, reminiscent of the many granite ledges of Rocky Narrows back in Sherborn.

Fishermen "read the water" when discerning currents and feeding lanes, and canoeists must do the same thing each time they choose a path around an obstruction. While the Charles has its share of obstructions and even the occasional quick-water run, it's really not much of a training ground for some of northern New England's more difficult rivers, whose rapids require instant decisions that had better be correct. I've canoed a few of those northern rivers, and they are exciting. But the relaxation found in "going with the flow," albeit a slow flow on the Charles, has its own advantages. The main one is simply the opportunity for unhurried observation, which is a rare commodity these days.

The Needham stretch of the Charles always reminds me of the experience my friend Dale Queenan and I had on a pond near the river. We had been bottom fishing with worms, and just as we decided to pack up our gear and head home my rod was suddenly pulled into the water. After I grabbed it, it became clear that either a large carp or a snapper had taken my bait. The beast easily stripped off my six-pound-test, and the drag on my reel started making sounds I'd never heard before. The speed of the outflowing line convinced me it was a carp.

*The bridge to Elm Bank Reservation; ahead lie miles of woods and coves.*

Normally, I side with the majority of anglers who feel that carp are trash fish, but now that I had one on, and a big one at that, my opinion changed—I wanted that fish. A million questions raced through my mind, the most urgent ones being: (1) Could I turn him before all my line was gone? (2) How long would I have to play him before he tired? (3) How the hell am I going to land such a heavy fish? and (4) What would I do with him once I landed him?

Question one answered itself: the carp swam to the middle of the pond and then just cruised back and forth. Skipping to question three: I decided that Dale should try to scoop up the carp using a combination of our small trout net and his arms. As you can imagine, he wasn't too wild about the idea, but a small crowd of spectators had gathered, and Dale felt obliged to do his part.

Now, to question two: how long should I play this fish? Well, after I'd spent a full twenty-five minutes inching the carp toward shore, the spectators were starting to grumble about the slow progress. They wanted to see this monster landed before dark. Just as Dale felt their pressure, I was influenced by their remarks, and I started to rush things. Big mistake.

I worked the carp into about two feet of water and figured he was tired enough for Dale to handle. It was now or never—and it turned out to be never. Dale waded into the water and managed to get his hands around the fish briefly before they both disappeared in a spray of water. Then my line snapped and so did Dale's patience. The fish was gone, Dale marched to the car, and the crowd booed my poor performance—the same crowd that two minutes earlier demanded that I hurry up and land the fish because they wanted to go home.

At least I learned some lessons for the future: (1) Carp really are trash fish, beneath the attention of an angler like myself—avoid them whenever possible; (2) crowds are fickle—avoid them at all costs, especially when fishing; and (3) don't ask friends to do the impossible, and if you do, avoid them for at least two weeks!

## Recreation Guide

# South Natick to Dedham

## PADDLING

*One Car*: Centre Street/Central Avenue on the Dover-Needham line is a good place to put in and head upstream. (There is a small parking pull-off on the Needham side of the bridge.) A paddle through the upstream marshes and coves provides good bird-watching and excellent bass and pickerel fishing.

*Two Cars*: The Elm Bank Reservation in Wellesley has a launching area. The reservation is open Wednesday through Sunday. (Please keep the area clean.) You could launch from here and leave a car waiting at the Centre Street/Central Avenue bridge on the Dover-Needham line. Consider bringing a topographical map so you won't get lost in the many coves. About five miles: no portages.

## RIVER WALKS

The Charles River Peninsula may be small at twenty-nine acres, but that's fine because hardly anyone knows about this spot. The property protects a mile of frontage on the Charles and offers excellent wildlife watching in the fields and small patches of brush and woods. It is accessible by both canoe (north bank of the river) and by car (Fisher Street in Needham).

Elm Bank Reservation has one of the finest river walks found in the state. A river trail follows the edge of the peninsula for about a mile and a half.

*Kayaker in Needham rapids.*

## BIKING

This is a wonderful (and popular) bicycling route because of the scenic countryside, relatively quiet back roads, and many interesting points of interest along the way. The total ride is 7.1 miles, but this can easily be extended by following the other side roads shown on the map.

The ride begins at the Village Falls Park at the Cochrane Dam on the Needham side of the river, where there is a parking lot near the bridge. From the parking lot turn left and follow Willow Street over the river and past a marsh to Cross Street at 0.7 mile. Turn right on Cross Street and follow it for 0.5 mile to its end. Go right on Centre Street for 0.3 mile and then turn left on Claybrook Street.

Claybrook Street is one of those special New England country lanes that are becoming all too rare in eastern Massachusetts. It passes by woods, streams, handsome houses, and a couple of farms, with an occasional glimpse of the Charles. About 1.3 miles down the road you pass over the mouth of Trout Brook which feeds the Charles, and then a bit farther Claybrook crosses Main Street and finally ends at Pleasant Street roughly 1.7 miles from its beginning. Turn right here, passing (or stopping at) Marino's Lookout Farm which has hillside apple orchards for picking your own apples in the autumn. Be on the lookout for Dover Road on the right about 0.5 mile down Pleasant Street, where our ride turns. However, you might want to go straight on Pleasant Street for a quarter-mile to rest at the South Natick Dam, where there are benches and picnic tables overlooking the waterfall.

Dover Road will take you back toward your car. It is a straight road that passes by estates, meadows, and forested hills. The Ridge Hill Reservation is about 1.9 miles down the road and makes a nice rest stop, with sunny fields bordering woodlands. When you have traveled 2.5 miles on Dover Road you should take caution crossing Central Street and continue on Dover Road another 0.5 mile to South Street. Turn right on South Street and in a couple hundred feet you are back at your car at the Village Falls Park. Take a few moments to explore the field above the dam and to cruise down scenic Mill Street past the rapids in the river or ride up Fisher Street to check out the launch site at Redwing Bay.

## BIRDING

The stretch of the Charles from Redwing Bay to Trout Brook has been a particularly good birding spot for me, with wood ducks, kestrels, cardinals, marsh wrens, and many black-crowned night herons spotted over the years. The Charles River Peninsula offers good viewing for kestrels, red-tailed hawks, sharp-shinned hawks, and bluebirds, which frequent the open fields.

One of my most memorable birding experiences occurred here when I had my fifteen seconds of fame while shooting the television show *Chronicle* for an episode titled "The Hidden Charles." The cameraman and I had spent a whole day on the river looking for wildlife with little success. We saw many of the more common birds such as Canada geese, great blue herons, and a kingfisher that seemed to stay just out of clear camera view for most of the trip. The cameraman was filming me paddling, when something very odd occurred right behind him. A great blue heron flew across the river followed by a red-tailed hawk that swooped down on the heron and pecked it, causing the heron to falter in flight for a moment as it let out a deep noise that could be described only as a croak. Of course the whole incident was over in a matter of seconds, and we never did get it on film. But I relive the scene every time I paddle around the bend in the river where it happened.

## ANGLING

Largemouth bass and carp all over the river; pickerel in the setbacks. Trout at the South Natick Dam.

## PICNICKING

Elm Bank Reservation, the Charles River Peninsula, and Village Falls/Cochrane Dam area. Farther from the Charles there is picnicking at Oak Grove Farm on Route 115 in Millis and Noanet Woodlands on Dedham Road in Dover.

## POINTS OF HISTORIC INTEREST
Explore the remains of the mill dating back to the 1800s at the Cochrane Dam—bring your camera—rapids and waterfall!

## CANOE RENTAL
Tropicland Marine & Tackle
100 Bridge Street, Dedham
617-329-3777

Directions: From Route 128 take Route 109 east into Dedham; Tropicland will be on the right side of the road.

# 6

# Twists and Turns along Route 128

S HOULD THE RESIDENTS of eastern Massachusetts be asked to trace the path of the Charles, my guess is that 90 percent would mistakenly draw a fairly straight line in a northeasterly direction, moving from the western suburbs towards Boston. Logic would dictate that the river should first cross Route 128 somewhere in the vicinity of Weston. That would be too simple for the Charles. It seems the river wants to make its mark on as many towns as possible before spilling into the sea.

The Charles actually crosses Route 128 three times before finally taking an easterly course into Boston. The river first flows under Route 128 at the Needham-Dedham line, just north of Westwood. It then flows south for a few miles into Dedham, where it makes an abrupt turn back to the north. The flow moves northward for several miles to the Wellesley-Newton line, where the river crosses Route 128 again—and this time heads back to the west for a mile! The Charles reminds me of a lost driver, so confused that he's about to pack it in and go back home. But finally, as if handed a map, the Charles commits itself toward the bay and crosses Route 128 near the Massachusetts Turnpike at the

*Long Ditch in Dedham, constructed in 1654 by the early settlers.*

*Twists and Turns along Route 128* ••• 111

crosses Route 128 near the Massachusetts Turnpike at the Weston-Newton line. No shortcuts for this river.

The Charles offers one of the last natural settings within the noose of Route 128. I recall getting stuck in traffic on "America's Technology Highway" where the highway passes over the river at the Dedham line. Gazing upstream, I saw a great blue heron slowly flying toward me, using the river as its highway. As it crossed high above my car, it occurred to me that we were both going about our business—except the heron was moving and I wasn't.

After the Charles crosses under Route 128, it hugs Needham Street as it rolls into Dedham. One might expect that after so many miles of travel, the river would be twice as wide as it was back in Franklin, but, surprisingly, it appears about the same size as when it exited Populatic Pond. I could cast a lure from one bank to the other.

This Dedham stretch is a study in contradictions: one minute I can paddle through a quiet marsh, while the next my senses are assaulted by nearby roads, houses, and businesses. I once assumed the Charles simply wasn't worth canoeing here because of its proximity to Route 1, with its traffic and commercial buildings. Yet all is not lost: there are broad marshlands scattered among the developed areas—a canoeist simply has to take the good with the bad. The first couple of miles downstream from Needham Street are especially nice as the river snakes its way through marsh and woods. Another option is to canoe the Long Ditch, if the water is high enough. The ditch bypasses the entire Dedham loop (about four and a half miles of river), exiting the Charles along Needham Street well before the river reaches the commercial zone.

I've canoed Long Ditch only once and that was at the end of May, when the water was high enough to float my canoe but the current was slow enough to allow me to paddle back up it at the end of my trip. There is one portion of the ditch that flows perfectly straight—quite a contrast to the

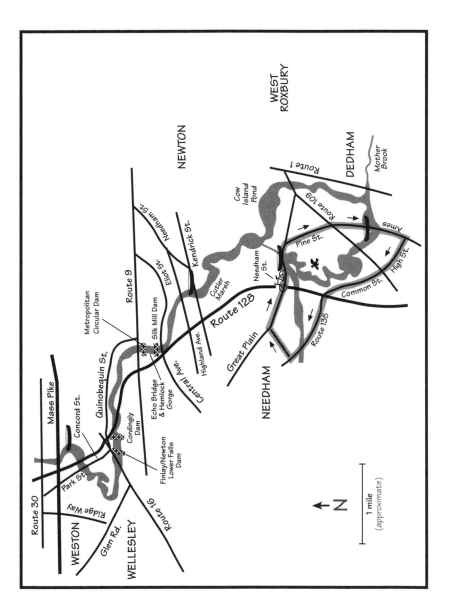

**ALONG ROUTE 128**

Charles. The banks are high and the marsh grass tall, so I really couldn't see much on either side, but that only adds to the intimate and solitary feeling I had from being in the heart of a large swamp. The width of the ditch is perhaps fifteen feet, and I wondered how on earth the settlers excavated it.

When I've canoed by Long Ditch in the summer it hasn't looked as inviting, and I figured it wasn't worth venturing deep into Cutler Marsh only to find my way blocked by an obstruction or shallow water. If I really want to see the south end of the marsh, I launch farther downstream near Cow Island Pond. But the ditch is still interesting. It's strange to see water being sucked out of the Charles by a stream, rather than having the stream replenish the river. In the springtime, water races out of the Charles over the shallow rocks beneath Needham Street, then continues rolling down Long Ditch through wetlands and enters the Charles farther downstream.

Long Ditch supposedly was dug to prevent flooding of some of Dedham's lowlands. Constructed in 1654, it is just one of the ways man has altered the flow of the river. The ditch actually makes a small part of Dedham into an island.

If I could turn back the clock and preserve one single area in a natural state it would be the Dedham loop. This peninsula (or island, if you count Long Ditch) would have made a perfect wildlife reservation, similar to the Charles River Peninsula in Needham but on a much larger scale. Instead, we have a massive commercial and residential area situated all too close to the river. Stanley Buzarewicz remembers this region as it was in the 1930s: "You never saw so much wildlife: pheasants, minks, otters, you name it. Where the front door of Lechmere's department store now stands was the exact spot where I caught five minks out of the same stump. That used to be a beautiful marsh."

Should you elect to canoe the Dedham Loop, you will have the pleasure of first seeing the handsome grounds of the Noble and Greenough School. At this point, the Charles spills into Motley Pond. A rather odd contrast in names: Noble School located on Motley Pond (perhaps the parents named the school, while the students named the pond).

Be prepared to have your peace and quiet interrupted by the roar of cars on Route 1. It is in this area that one of the river's strangest features lies—Mother Brook. This man-made brook (more like a canal) diverts a sizable portion of the Charles into the Neponset River to the south. Stanley told me that where the Charles and the Neponset come nearest to each other in Dedham was an area frequented by Indians; from this area they could easily reach either of the river highways.

One group of Indians rarely discussed are the Paleo-Indians, the first known people to inhabit New England roughly 10,000 years ago. The Paleo-Indian presence has been documented in Massachusetts, and it is likely that their hunting parties went up the Charles. In this postglacial period, the Indians hunted incredibly large animals, using spears tipped with stone points with grooved or fluted bases. One such animal, the mastadon, an elephant-like creature, could feed twenty Indians for three months. What a strange and different world the Charles must have flowed through! There were even giant beaver up to six feet long—imagine bumping into one of those while canoeing!

Tropicland Marine & Tackle is located next to the Charles in Dedham and is owned by Larry Mathews, an avid bass fisherman. Larry rents canoes which can be launched right behind the store. "The largemouth fishing," says Larry, "is excellent, with spinner baits and rubber worms at the top of my list for lures. The bridges, rock, and brush piles are all good spots to try, but the bass are everywhere. Cow Island Pond has a bunch of pickerel lurking in the weeds, and occasionally a trout is caught in the river, having made its way downstream all the way from South Natick."

I recall other Dedham anglers, such as Bill Brigham, giving similar reports of good fishing and commenting on

*The ditch passes through the heart of Cutler Marsh where the tall marsh grass, growing in the flat floodplains, makes you feel like you're in a Kansas prairie.*

116 ••• *Exploring the Hidden Charles*

wildlife along the river, even within the ring of Route 128. "I've seen deer and foxes, and one morning an owl swooped down and almost took my hat off," said Bill. His favorite lure is a spinner bait, and he thinks gravel-bottomed areas are among the most productive spots, especially during low-water periods. He once landed an eight-pounder from the Charles, so I think I better try spinner baits before Cogs catches the first lunker.

Although the bass can grow quite large in this area, most fish found in rivers never get quite as big as the same species does in a lake. I'm not sure why—surely the river fish get as much to eat as their lake-bound cousins. Perhaps the river current requires them to expend extra energy in day-to-day living. That may be one reason why "bulges" in the river, which have minimal currents, often have the best fishing. Most anglers are interested in the weight of a fish, but they should consider the fight as well. Lean, strong river fish put up a great fight.

Farther down the Charles lies Havey Beach and Playground, followed by Cow Island Pond, one of the river's biggest "bulges." On my last visit to Cow Island Pond, they must have put the cows in the barn and rolled up the island, because I saw neither. What I did see was a wide expanse of water covered with sea gulls, reminding me more of the ocean than the Charles. Looking downstream, however, where the river exits the pond, I saw a more familiar sight—meadows and marsh. This is the beginning of enormous Cutler Park, quite similar to the great Millis-Medfield Marsh I know so well. Cutler Park's wetlands stretch into parts of Dedham, Newton, and Needham on the west side of the Charles.

The Metropolitan District Commission says that Cutler Park is the largest freshwater marsh on the middle Charles. The park's six hundred acres extend all the way from Cow Island Pond to Kendrick Street in Needham. The wetlands offer excellent bird-watching, particularly in the spring. I especially enjoy searching for the hidden spots within the marsh—I guess it's my Huckleberry Finn–like love of exploration that makes it so appealing.

Upon exiting Cow Island Pond, the river soon meets the end of Long Ditch near a railroad bridge. The barren hill to the right on the other side of the bridge is the old Boston landfill, situated much too close to the river. There is a very shallow stretch of river here, and I would not be surprised if it's due to dirt eroding from the landfill and sliding into the Charles. Around the next bend, a ridge of trees on the right screens a number of cemeteries located just beyond view. Someday, we might want to consider having cemeteries double as public parks. Without headstones, they could be open fields.

The distant dull roar of Route 128 can be heard in the Cutler Park marsh when the wind is coming from the west. The highway is far enough away, however, that the noise is barely audible and does not overshadow the bird songs. There is no significant current here; in fact, a strong wind could actually push a canoe upstream. The river alternately narrows and widens as it twists through the marsh.

In some places, there are points of land with trees right at the water's edge. These are usually the best spots to find bass, because there are probably submerged trees or limbs on the river bottom. Features like these are known as "structure" to bass fishermen; such structure attracts minnows, which, in turn, attract bass. Also, a fallen tree provides cover from the sun, where really big bass often hide in ambush, waiting for prey.

Kendrick Street roughly marks the end of the Cutler Park marsh. Ahead lies a mixed bag of dams, residential areas, industrial sites, and an occasional patch of swamp. I'm personally not too enthusiastic about canoeing this area because of the development near Highland Avenue on the Newton-Needham line and also because of the many dams one must portage: the Silk Mill Dam, the Metropolitan Cir-

*Silk Mill Dam at Newton Upper Falls. Mills Falls Restaurant is perched high above the river.*

cular Dam, Cordingly Dam, and Finlay Dam at Newton Lower Falls. If you do attempt to canoe this stretch, I suggest purchasing a topographical map—the worst thing a canoiest can do is to set out not knowing exactly where these dangerous dams are.

This area is not without its charms. Hemlock Gorge is definitely worth seeing, but I prefer to drive there and explore by foot. The twenty-three-acre park is located off Central Avenue in Needham, just before it crosses over the river and into Newton, where it is called Eliot Street. Hemlock Gorge is the only steep canyon on the river—even Rocky Narrows cannot match its sheer slopes.

On a cold January morning, I made another visit to this wild area in the heart of suburbia. A six-inch cover of snow added to its beauty. An unusual variety of trees flourish here: hemlock, oak, mulberry, white pine, red pine, beech, birch, chestnut, and witch hazel all can be seen scattered on this rocky knoll. At the center of the park is the Silk Mill Dam, where the mighty Mill Falls (or Upper Falls) thunders down into the canyon below. The Mill Falls Restaurant sits perched high above the Charles—it looks like a great place to have a beer and watch the river flex its muscle.

The ancient and massive Echo Bridge offers a good view of the river, the falls, and the gorge. The MDC's *Reservations and Facilities Guide* details the hstory of this National Historic Landmark, saying, "When built in 1877 the bridge was the second-largest masonry arch in the United States." The bridge, made of brick and granite, rises far above the river, and if you are not wild about heights, stick to the park. Another entrance to Echo Bridge lies off Chestnut Street in Newton, where you can climb to the top. Below the bridge is a small platform where the echoes formed by the bridge really do sound impressive.

Just beyond Echo Bridge lies the unique, half-moon-shaped Metropolitan Circular Dam. For years I had driven along this stretch of Route 9 and never realized the dam lay

*Massive Echo Bridge, built in 1877, spans Hemlock Gorge.*

in its shadow, hidden between busy Route 9 and the end of Hemlock Gorge. The whole area is known as Newton Upper Falls, settled in 1681. A historic marker near the dam calls Upper Falls "an Early American Industrial Village," another of the early mill sites along the Charles.

On the north side of Route 9, the Charles follows a northerly course wedged between Route 128 on the left and a narrow strip of MDC parkland on the right. Also on the right is Quinobequin Street, named after the Indian word for the river. (I've found two spellings of this Indian term— Quineboquin and Quinebequin. Some historians think Quineboquin was actually the name of Maine's Kennebec River and was mistakenly applied to the Charles when old maps were misread.) It is possible to go for a short canoe ride here before reaching the falls at Cordingly Dam. However, in some places the river passes so close to Route 128 that you not only hear the steady stream of traffic, you can see it as well.

You don't have to canoe a river to enjoy it; I've walked, jogged, bicycled, and fished along Quinobequin Street. Occasionally, I see wildlife in the parkland, and it was here that I was robbed by a raccoon. Early one evening many years ago, I was fishing from shore, hoping to catch a couple of bass for dinner. After landing my first fish, I placed it on a patch of grass behind me. A raccoon caught a whiff of it, and he, too, decided to have bass for dinner. The masked bandit shuffled down the hill, picked up the fish (just ten feet from where I stood), and quickly dragged his meal away. He showed absolutely no fear of me, and I elected not to tangle with so bold a thief.

The next area worth exploring is Newton Lower Falls, where both Cordingly and Finlay Dams are located on the Newton-Wellesley border. While Finlay Dam is a popular spot for viewing the river, the natural falls by Cordingly Dam lie hidden between commercial buildings and often go undiscovered. But Cordingly is worth the search: rushing water

*Cordingly Dam, footbridge, and fish ladder (Newton-Wellesley).*

cascades over rock ledge into the rapids below, forming one of the most picturesque sites on the river. Best of all, spanning the river is a footbridge that connects Wellesley with Newton. After a heavy rain, the sight of white churning water and the sounds of the roaring falls make a walk over the footbridge a special treat. The dam is located behind Walnut Office Park on Walnut Street, just a short distance from Route 128 in Wellesley.

The better-known Finlay Dam is located just a few hundred feet downstream from Cordingly. I once worked nearby, and on lunch breaks I would go down to the dam and watch the construction of the fishway. Visions of migrating shad swimming through the fishway (or fish ladder) gave the project a real sense of excitement, especially for an avid angler like myself.

The shad is an anadromous game fish that spawns in the rivers each spring. I've caught them from both the Connecticut River and the South Shore's North River. These fish always give an exciting fight, and presumably they strike a lure like a shad dart out of anger or a sense of territorial defense during the spawn. I've found that they strike with even more vigor during the early evening and night. A hundred years ago, shad was an important part of the New England diet, and harvesting shad in the springtime was an annual event.

Although the MDC has no immediate plans to expand the fishways, I think it would be an important project in restoring the Charles to its proper role in fisheries habitat. I have hopes that someday I'll be supplementing my bass and trout catch with migrating shad. Once the various fish ladders are built, including a new one at the South Natick Dam, the shad will have a clear shot to my doorstep sixty miles upstream.

Good canoeing begins again beyond Finlay Dam. The Charles winds its way through the Leo J. Martin Memorial Golf Course, offering a quiet setting away from major roadways. There are a number of coves to explore, and once again the marshes and woods provide good bird and wildlife viewing. The open feeling created by the surrounding golf course reminds me of a canoeing scene done in watercolors by Winslow Homer entitled *The Blue Boat*. Although the colors are similar to Monet's *Branch of the Seine*, the painting is entirely different, with a more earthy, New England feeling.

In winter, good cross-country skiing can be had at the golf course, with just about every accommodation and accessory available, including lighted trails, rental equipment, skiing lessons, and refreshments. During the warm-weather months, this public course provides fine golfing. I've tried my luck there a number of times and have learned that the Charles does indeed have a strong hold on me—that's where most of my shots land.

A short distance downstream, between the grid of highway entrance and exit ramps, is a small oasis called Recreation Park. The park is located on the banks of the Charles and has an open field and a small walking bridge extending over the river. If you wish to canoe the golf course, you could launch here and paddle upstream. The park is located just off the Recreation Road exit on Route 128.

Recreation Park was another one of my old lunch-break haunts. I recall sitting at the edge of the large field there one afternoon, watching a flock of starlings pick through the grass. Out of the corner of my eye, I saw a rust-colored bird glide by and perch on the branch of a nearby tree. The bird looked like a miniature red-tailed hawk, but its size and coloring told me it was an American kestrel. The starlings showed no concern over this little member of the falcon family—either they didn't see the kestrel or, perhaps, they didn't care. But they should have.

After a few minutes of sitting quietly, the kestrel attacked and frightened starlings flew every which way. The kestrel had already chosen its target, and when the victim was only six feet off the ground, the speeding kestrel slammed into it. In a spray of black feathers, both birds tumbled to the earth. For a second it appeared as if the starling might escape, but the kestrel pounced on it, and that was that.

This was the first time I'd seen a kestrel kill another bird. They are better known for hunting insects and small rodents, and I've seen them along the Charles perched on tree limbs or telephone wires. I've also spotted them hovering over a field, searching for grasshoppers or mice.

Here at the end of the suburban stretch of the Charles, the river is in transition. Nature clings on stubbornly, but more and more roads, houses, and people crowd the river. The kestrel I saw was perched in the very shadow of the Mass Pike and Route 128. Millions of people drive by this part of the Charles, but few see the river and fewer know it. For me, the exploration of this developed area has been a pleasant surprise—there are still some pockets of natural beauty, and a few of the many man-made features, such as Echo Bridge, enhance rather than detract from the Charles.

As the river enters Waltham, the waters fan out and the current slows to a crawl. Like some weekend athlete attempting to run the Boston Marathon, which also begins in Hopkinton, the river limps toward the finish line in Boston.

Ahead lie the last few miles of the river, different from anything we have seen to this point.

# Twists and Turns along Route 128

## PADDLING

*One Car:* Park at the Kendrick Street bridge on the Needham-Newton town line and paddle upstream to enter the vast Cutler Park marsh. If you elect to go downstream through the woods, you have about a half-mile of peaceful paddling before approaching the highly developed towns of Needham and Newton. This stretch is also somewhat dangerous, as there are a series of dams ahead with little space for pulling out. I do not recommend going beyond a half-mile downstream from Kendrick Street.

*Two Cars:* Leave one car at Kendrick Street on the Needham-Newton line, then drive to the intersection of Route 109 and Route 1 in Dedham where Route 109 crosses the river south of Cow Island Pond. From here you can canoe back to Kendrick Street. It's a long paddle through open marsh, so avoid windy or scorching hot days. Bring plenty of supplies. About five miles; no portages.

## RIVER WALKS

Hemlock Gorge is a great place for a short stroll in the heart of suburbia. The property includes the Silk Mill Dam (Mills Falls), Echo Bridge, and the Metropolitan Circular Dam. This little knob of land has a variety of interesting trees and plants, but my favorite are the majestic hemlocks, which are not all that common in this area. The property is managed by the MDC and there is parking on Central Avenue in

Needham. You can extend your walk by crossing Route 9 to Quinobequin Street.

While you are in the area, consider visiting the falls and footbridge at Cordingly Dam (behind the commercial buildings on Route 16, just east of the Finlay Dam. Another entrance to Cordingly Dam is behind Walnut Office Park on Walnut Street.)

Another spot to explore by foot is the Needham Pathway, constructed by the MDC. It runs from Kendrick Street (where there is parking at Nahanant Park) to Highland Avenue, a distance of about three-fourths of a mile. You can also make a short bike ride along the river here on a paved path that connects with Fourth Avenue, paralleling the river.

## BIKING

As the river enters the inside ring of Route 128 the roads become more congested, and bicycling is most enjoyable during periods of low traffic such as early on Saturday and Sunday mornings. The loop ride for this chapter is a relatively short ride of 6.6 miles through Dedham and Needham.

The ride begins on Needham Street just east of Route 128 where there is parking off the road near a metal gate on the right. Follow Needham Street toward Dedham, paralleling the river and passing over Long Ditch to Pine Street, which is 0.7 mile from the start. Go right on Pine Street, passing the Noble and Greenough School. Private homes line the left side of the street and woods are on the right. At 0.8 mile down Pine Street it crosses Route 109 (caution) and the road turns into Ames Street. You will cross the Charles at a bridge near a side road called Pleasant Street that was once the site of a boathouse.

Proceed 0.5 mile down Ames Street to a stoplight and turn right on High Street. Go 0.5 mile on High Street, passing by many large houses, until you reach a stoplight at a village green lined with a granite and rail fence. Proceed straight through the stop sign; the road now becomes Common Street. You will pass Wilson Mountain Reservation on the left about a mile down Common Street, and then at about 1.4 miles stay left and continue on Route 135/West Street. Follow Route 135 for an additional 1.4 miles passing beneath Route 128 and over the Charles until you come to South Street, where you should turn right. South Street is a quiet back road. In 0.7 mile South Street will bring you to Great Plain Avenue, where you should turn right. A short cruise of 0.6 mile will bring you back to your car.

## BIRDING

My favorite spots for birding include the area just upstream of Motley Pond, the Long Ditch and Cow Island Pond area, the Cutler Park marsh, and the stretch of river that runs by the Leo J. Martin Memorial Golf Course. Great blue herons, green-backed herons, and black-crowned night herons are seen along the water's edge, while in the riverside trees and brush look for marsh wrens, cardinals, warblers, woodpeckers, and the occasional wood duck. Waterfowl is common in the broad expanses of the Cutler Park marsh.

## ANGLING

Largemouth bass and carp all over the river, bullheads on the slow water, pickerel in the setbacks and in Cow Island Pond, and northern pike in the Lakes District.

## PICNICKING

The best picnicking is at Hemlock Gorge in Needham, and Recreation Park in Weston.

## POINTS OF HISTORIC INTEREST
• Canoe up Long Ditch, constructed in 1654.
• Explore Hemlock Gorge and view massive Echo Bridge, Mills Falls, and the Circular Dam.

## CANOE & KAYAK RENTAL
Charles River Canoe & Kayak Service
2401 Commonwealth Ave., Newton
617-965-5110

Tropicland Marine & Tackle
100 Bridge Street, Dedham
617-329-3777


Directions: On Commonwealth Avenue (Route 30) near the Weston town line, just east of the Massachusetts Turnpike. Adjacent to the Newton Marriott Hotel.

# 7

# The Lakes District to the Boston University Bridge

THE FINAL LEG of the Charles before Boston starts at Norumbega, at the junction of Route 128 and the Mass Pike where Commonwealth Avenue abuts the river. Because of the Moody Street dam, located downstream, the Charles here spreads into an impoundment and is more like a lake than a river. Appropriately enough, the area is referred to as the Lakes District.

The headquarters of the Charles River Watershed Association is located here. I have the hard-working members of the CRWA to thank for my countless hours of pleasure on the Charles. Without their coordinated efforts, I doubt the river's recent renewal would have ever ocurred. Perhaps the most important work of the association has been their steady effort to recruit volunteers to defend the river. It's really rather ironic: we used to defend ourselves from nature, and now we defend nature from ourselves.

The CRWA has been active in many important initiatives to improve the health of the Charles. One is known informally as the "Disconnection Project," which the EPA initiated in an effort to identify illegally connected sewer lines that are discharging into storm drains without

*Because of the Moody Street dam the Charles spreads into an impoundment and is more like a lake than a river. This area is referred to as the Lakes District.*

132 • • • *Exploring the Hidden Charles*

treatment. The project encompasses ten towns along the lower part of the Charles and is in support of the "Clean Charles 2005 Initiative," which seeks to secure a swimmable/fishable lower Charles by Earth Day 2005. To date, the program has been largely successful, with many illegal connections already disconnected from storm drains and properly channeled toward sewage treatment plants.

Another project the CRWA is monitoring is the Combined Sewer Overflow Project proposed by the MWRA, which is making recommendations to update the antiquated sewer infrastructure in Boston and Cambridge. Unlike most cities, some areas of Boston and Cambridge use the same sewer system for both runoff and sewage, rather than separate pipes. In simple terms this means that when big storms occur sewer pipes overflow, diverting their mix of rainwater and untreated or partially treated sewage directly into the Charles. While actual implementation of the recommendations may take years, recent court orders and oversight by the EPA ensure that this problem eventually will be resolved.

In a recent conversation with Bob Zimmerman, executive director of the CRWA, he pointed out that the three major problems facing the river—combined sewer overflow, low flow/draw-offs, and non-point-source pollution—are "really symptoms of a bigger problem: the way we engineer our communities. We design towns to get the water out of town as fast as possible, but we really should reverse that trend, by slowing the water down. There are many things we could do, such as bringing back storm-water retention ponds and taking tributaries out of pipes to let them run naturally through wetlands. Even homeowners can take the water that runs off their roofs and collect it in cisterns to use for the garden." Zimmerman pointed out other successful strategies like the Natural Valley Storage Areas that preserve wetlands along the river to absorb and store flood waters. Wetlands work much more effectively than levies that merely channel the water in constricted passages. Eventually, during really major storms, the levies are breached or the water is channeled downstream to undiked areas which flood.

When I first met Bob several years ago he was battling early plans referred to as the Scheme Z proposal regarding the construction of Boston's new Central Artery highway, which would have dashed MDC and CRWA's commitment to providing continuous parkland along the lower Charles River Basin. I could not help but compare Scheme Z to another detrimental proposal from an earlier time. In 1907, architect Ralph Adams Cram submitted plans to build an island in the middle of the basin, in which to create more space for development. Fortunately, the proposal was never carried out. My hunch is that if Bob Zimmerman and the CRWA had been around at that time, they would have battled that proposal with the same energy they offer today in protection of the river.

The Norumbega region is a popular spot—on the left is a duck feeding station and farther downstream in the Charles River Reservation is Norumbega Tower. This 110-foot tower marks where the Vikings are said to have built a fort long before Columbus "discovered" America. Historians generally agree that the Norsemen sailed along the coast; however, whether the Vikings ventured inland along the Charles is open to debate. There has been no scientific substantiation of the theory. Similar debates continue regarding other supposed Viking sites, such as the area near South End Pond in Millis, where mysterious trenches have been found.

On the right side of the river is a canoe rental facility run by the Charles River Canoe & Kayak Service. Many folks take their first paddle on the river here. Also on the east bank is the sprawling Marriott Hotel, once the site of the world-famous Norumbega Park.

In the late 1800s and through the first part of the 1900s, Norumbega Park was a premier social and recreation spot, both day and night. My mother-in-law, Helen Carty, remembers it from her many visits during the 1940s: "That

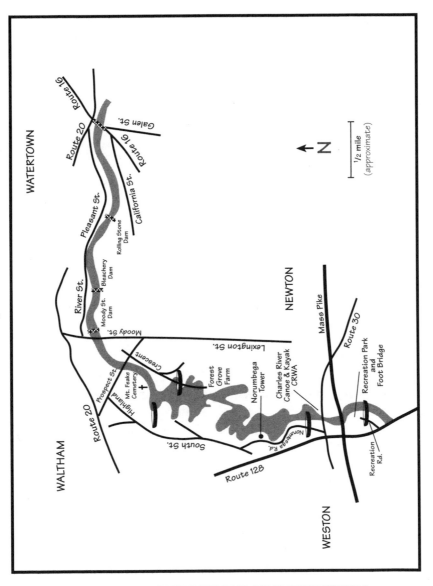

**LAKES DISTRICT TO WATERTOWN**

was the place to go; couples or stag, it didn't matter, so long as they dressed properly. We would dance to the big bands, like Tommy Dorsey or Artie Shaw, who performed in the beautiful dance hall. And during the day we would picnic by the river, watching boats and canoes. Those were the days— and Norumbega was a spot and a half!"

With a glowing description like that, it's easy for me to imagine a midnight canoe ride with my date, while the big-band sounds wafted out over the water. What a wonderful place it must have been, even for children, who could visit the park's zoo or enjoy a pedal-boat or canoe ride with their parents. I actually get jealous when I realize that my generation will never have a place like Norumbega.

Local historian Robert Pollock is the real expert on Norumbega Park and its famous Totem Pole Ballroom. He has prepared an excellent slide show chronicling the park, with interesting details of its history: "Presidents from Coolidge to Kennedy visited Norumbega, and virtually every swing band performed at the Totem Pole, along with entertainers like Frank Sinatra, Sammy Davis Jr., Frankie Laine, Teresa Brewer, and Pat Boone." Mr. Pollock went on to tell me that literally millions of people from the greater Boston area visited Norumbega and millions more danced at the Totem Pole. One of the most interesting facts this historian uncovered was that "when the Commonwealth Avenue Street Railway Company opened Norumbega in 1897, there were only twenty-four houses on Commonwealth Avenue between Boston and Weston. The trolley line between Lake Street in Brighton and Norumbega Park brought about the land development and greatly increased the real estate values along Commonwealth Avenue." Today, there are homes filling almost every available open space on both sides of the road.

I found an advertisement for the park from the 1950s, with directions "via the new Route 128 Super-Highway." Now, when was the last time you heard the term superhighway applied to Route 128?

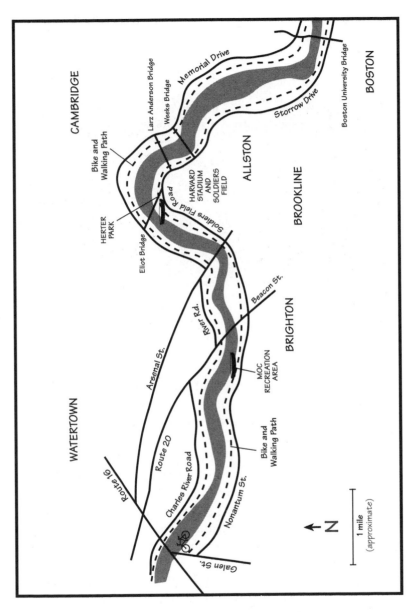

# WATERTOWN TO B.U. BRIDGE

*Norumbega Park, a premier recreational and social spot at the end of the nineteenth century, is unequaled on the Charles today.* Photo courtesy of the Charles River Watershed Association.

Inside the headquarters of the CRWA is an old photograph of the Norumbega Boathouse, which was located at about the spot where the Marriott now stands. The picture shows hundreds of canoes (with women holding parasols) gathered for the "5th Annual Gala Day" held in 1919. It is ironic that while most recreation spots become more crowded over time, this part of the Charles now sees far fewer people. Before the automobile, there were a number of boathouses in Newton, two more in Natick, and others in Cambridge, Waltham, and Dedham. On a warm summer day there would be thousands of canoeists scattered along the river. Mr. Pollock estimates that, at the height of canoeing in the Lakes District, there were perhaps 5,000 canoes in the area. If they were lined up end to end along the river, they would have stretched from the Moody Street dam to Newton Lower Falls in three separate unbroken lines—more than seventeen miles of canoes! There may have been more canoeing done in these few miles than in any place in the world.

Downstream from Commonwealth Avenue, a canoeist could become a bit confused due to the area's many coves, some of which stretch for almost a half-mile. While there may not be the secluded feeling found on the upper Charles, the bordering parks and reservation lands do provide tranquil scenery and good habitat for ducks and other birds. But the river itself isn't serene, as motorboats appear from time to time, sending out wakes and engine noise. The atmosphere on this portion of the Charles is more befitting a popular lake. Its character has been transformed from shy loner to boisterous conventioneer. And although the river's water quality drops off a bit from the upper Charles, this region

*Safety patrols at Norumbega Park helped to ensure the safety of a great many river enthusiasts.* Photo courtesy of the Charles River Watershed Association.

does have its advantages, including great fishing for warm-water species.

The pickerel and bass must compete here with a much larger fish—the northern pike. The Massachusetts Division of Fisheries and Wildlife selected the perfect spot to stock these ferocious-looking monsters. The Lakes District offers excellent habitat for pike: shallow, weedy coves with a healthy supply of food in the form of panfish and baitfish. These toothy monsters will grow to more than twenty pounds, and the handful of anglers who know where to find them are having a ball. Few things are more exciting than trying to get one of these monsters in the boat, and, in fact, many anglers fail to do so. Ice fishermen often catch more pike than summertime anglers; the cold waters of winter can make the fish sluggish and easier to haul up. Pike can make strong runs even in the winter, however, and I've heard stories about pike splintering ice-fishing gear and dragging it right through the ice.

Fishermen entice the pike to strike with a combination of surface plugs, crank baits, spinner baits, spoons, jigs, rubber worms, and—perhaps most effective of all—five- or six-inch shiners, free to dart about and goad even the most wary pike into attacking. Anglers had better be equipped with heavy lines, wire leaders, and large nets if they expect to land one of the river's huge northerns. The Bear's Den Tackle Shop in Waltham seems to be the place to go for advice on catching northerns.

I can really feel the heartbeat of the river during the evening hours, especially within that brief transition period before darkness falls, when the water's surface is as smooth as glass. I was canoeing the Lakes District one evening last fall when the setting October sun cast a golden hue over the entire landscape. The scene was a brief one, and while my photos captured the visual effect, they don't really do it justice, because it was the sense of quiet and calm that made the moment special. I was reminded of Robert Frost's poem "October":

> O hushed October morning mild
> Begin the hour of this day slow
> Make the day seem to us less brief

It's during such moments of astounding beauty that I wish my canoe seat had a back, so I could recline and gaze upward. It wasn't until recently that I learned that the manufacturers of both my canoes (Old Town and Coleman) do make special backrests that work well. Actually, a wide range of canoe accessories are available, including wooden motor mounts for tiny electric motors.

Jon Cogswell and I recently canoed the Lakes District on a warm autumn Sunday morning, when people were enjoying the river for a variety of reasons. In the coves there were anglers in bass boats, probing the weed edge for largemouths and pike; along the shore, children were fishing with worms and bobbers; and on the docks and decks of the houses along the bank, folks were reading the paper with morning coffee.

Cogs and I had come to do battle with the northern pike in the Kingsbury Cove and Twin Coves, where some nice pike had been taken recently. While we were loading the canoe, Cogs chuckled when he saw my huge boat net; it looked like it was made for shark fishing. But, I figured, why take chances. I had never caught a large pike, and I didn't want to lose one just because we could not boat it. We proceeded to poke around coves and islands, pitching top-water plugs, bottom-bouncing lures, and everything in between. No luck, not even a hit. I'll never figure out fish—the day before, I was catching one bass after another upstream in Natick, and then a mere twenty-four hours later, not even a bite. Maybe it has something to do with the lunar alignment, who knows?

We didn't catch any pike or bass that day, yet we had a great day of fishing. The "fishing" part of fishing is just one of the sport's many aspects; an equally important part of fishing is being outdoors on the water, and if you have good company, it's all the better. Cogs and I talked for hours, cursed the pike, and talked some more. Conversation just seems to flow more easily when you are on the water, away from distractions. "Civilization is a limitless multiplication of unnecessary necessaries," said Mark Twain. How right he was—on the river, I can escape all the clutter of modern life and enjoy simple things like good conversation. It's nice to have a friend whose company I can enjoy no matter what I'm doing—and on that day, we weren't doing much of anything. Oh, yeah, we did get a nice picture of a muskrat who swam by our boat. Poor Cogs, I'm always dragging him along on a fishing excursion where we end up chasing a muskrat or some such nonsense—in fact, now that I think of it, it's been awhile since we actually caught any fish. Something will have to be done about that.

We paddled back to our car, parked at the duck feeding station at Norumbega. While unloading the canoe, Cogs picked up some discarded fishing line that had been left in the parking lot. Some anglers can be slobs, others, like Cogs, go out of their way to help keep the river and its environs clean. Long before environmentalism was fashionable, Cogs was picking up other people's trash and releasing most of the fish he caught. If the suburban/urban river is to survive the crush of people, we need outdoorspeople who leave the river in better shape than they find it. The northern pike had us "skunked," but we vowed to come back to Norumbega. Perhaps if we fished right below the Mass Pike, our luck would be better.

About a mile and a half downstream from Norumbega lie the last four coves of the Lakes District: Maple Cove, Purgatory Cove, Quinobequin Bay, and Crams Cove. On the right side of the river in Waltham, there is a small MDC park

*A view of the Lakes District from Mount Feake Cemetery. In the early 1900s, this portion of the Charles was jammed with canoes.*

called Forest Grove. It can be reached either by boat or by driving out on the peninsula via Woerd Avenue. The park has a nice pine grove perfect for shore fishing. Also on Woerd Avenue is an MDC boat launch. Brandeis University sits high above the river on the other side.

Just after the last cove, the Charles makes a sweeping curve before the Prospect Street bridge. On the left, commanding an excellent view of the river, is the Mount Feake Cemetery. The cemetery sprawls for quite a distance and pays its respects to the Charles with many lanes named after the river: Quinobequin, River, and River View Avenues. In the fall when the leaves are off the trees, climbing Mount Feake gives a fairly good view of the Charles as the river makes its way eastward into downtown Waltham.

At the Prospect Street bridge, the Charles begins its third and final transition, going from a suburban river to a city river. Houses and commercial buildings begin to crowd in, and the wide marshy coves of the Lakes District come to an abrupt end.

Though many people continue to canoe beyond Prospect Street, my paddling is over and my pedaling begins. I trade my canoe for a bicycle, because the many dams below turn canoeing from fun to work. Portaging a heavily loaded canoe is not my idea of a good time, especially when the portages are through parking lots, not wood lots.

Below Prospect Street there are four dams spanning the river in Waltham, Newton, and Watertown. Each dam lies about a mile from the last in the following order from west to east: Moody Street dam, Bleachery Dam, Rolling Stone Dam, and the Watertown Dam, which lies on the site of the first dam ever built on the Charles. While this area is highly developed, some wildlife hangs on. For example, at the confluence of Cheesecake Brook (who named that one?) and the Charles in Newton, there is a strip of woods along the right bank of the river. It's not exactly the best place to hike, but it does offer local residents a chance to see an assortment of birds, ducks, turtles, and even an occasional pheasant or cottontail.

Farther downstream, the strip of woods is replaced by grassy parkland, park benches, and even a footbridge spanning the river off California Street just above the Watertown Dam. This area of "the Great Dam at Watertown" had a footbridge spanning the river as early as 1634. The small park on the Newton side is a nice spot from which to view the river—you can sit on a bench and gaze at the smooth water above the dam or watch the rapids below. Just downstream is the beginning of the Dr. Paul Dudley White Charles River Bike Path, which follows the river through Newton, Watertown, Cambridge, and Boston.

The section of the river along North Beacon Street was an important settlement for American Indians and prehistoric tribes; cutting tools found here date back to 1600 B.C. At that time, the bay tides met the river in this vicinity. Some

*Early map of the Charles River: Waltham Watch Factory site.*
Photo courtesy of Charles River Watershed Association.

of the ancient artifacts found here are displayed at the Peabody Museum at Harvard University.

One of the more encouraging events along the Charles has been the continued expansion of the greenway along the banks of the river from Watertown Square through Watertown, Newton, Waltham, and Weston to Commonwealth Avenue. The project, known as the Charles River Restoration Project, was begun by the MDC in 1992 when the agency completed a survey that accurately delineated MDC-controlled land along the river. The survey identified ninety-two encroachments on MDC property within this area and confirmed that once the land was reclaimed by the MDC, there would be enough space to construct the greenway. Besides the obvious recreational potential of riverside paths, the greenway will enhance wildlife habitat, reduce non-point-source pollution entering the river, and provide people with an alternate way (such as biking) to commute into the city. When completed in the summer of 1998, the greenway will link the basin all the way upriver to the Lakes District—a wonderful use of riverfront property for all people to enjoy—and will give the Charles the distinction of having one of the longest urban river greenway corridors in America.

Dan Driscoll, senior planner for the MDC, reports that "eventually the goal is to extend the greenway from Weston and Newton into Needham and West Roxbury, connecting with Brook Farm. We have already made great progress. Due to the cooperation of abutters along Fourth Avenue we have opened the Needham Pathway from Kendrick Street to Highland Avenue."

"We have come full circle over the past one hundred years," Driscoll comments. "An initial period of resource protection, park development, and heavy public use was followed by decades of neglect, abuse, and lost public interest. Today the public's historic love for the Charles has reawakened, stimulating renewed desire to protect and restore the river and its banks."

*The ancient mills and factories of Waltham.*

One February day, the thermometer climbed all the way to fifty-eight degrees, and the parklands along the Charles in Newton and Watertown were full of people. I felt like the proverbial groundhog who, upon poking his head out of the burrow and finding the air warm, goes out for a quick stroll before winter weather returns. I had my binoculars with me and was watching a bright red cardinal feed along the river, when I noticed a bird-watcher standing on a sandbar just a few yards downstream. I took a picture of him because he happened to be standing at the first spot on the river where there is a view of the Boston skyline. I thought it a tribute to the Charles that we could have successful birding in the shadow of the city.

I introduced myself, and learned that the other man's name was Michael Griffin. He told me he occasionally walks down to the river equipped with binoculars and a camera with a telephoto lens, hoping to take the "perfect" picture. We compared notes on the birds we had seen here over the years, and Mike surprised me by saying that during the summer months a great blue heron frequented the sandbar we were standing on.

Some of the other interesting birds Mike had spotted along the Newton-Watertown stretch of the Charles included common mergansers, hooded mergansers, double-crested cormorants, and belted kingfishers. Not a bad representation of birdlife for an area just six or seven miles from the heart of the city. I doubt that many other metropolitan areas the size of Boston could boast of a river with the wildlife diversity of the Charles. Even my favorite stretch from Norfolk to Natick, with its deer, otters, and trout is only a thirty-to-forty-five-minute drive from the city.

Mike mentioned that he had seen a number of cormorants, which might be common in Watertown but are rarely spotted upstream, away from the ocean. These large birds are incredible swimmers; like loons, they can chase fish underwater. The merganser is also a fish-eating duck that can dive underwater, but the smaller hooded merganser is rather uncommon. Kingfishers are well established all over New England, and if you spot a slate blue bird with a rather large head and long beak, flying straight down the middle of the Charles, there's a good chance it's a kingfisher.

Along Nonantum and North Beacon Streets the river begins to widen, and the Newton and Watertown Yacht Clubs are located here. This marks the first area on the Charles where large powerboats are moored, and a canoe ride through here may not be very relaxing. On a sunny summer weekend, both the river and the bike paths are packed; it seems this area of the river gets overused, while the upper Charles remains underutilized—but I'm not complaining. I like the fact that the upper river is hidden and there are enough river miles to keep visitors widely dispersed. In fact, people throughout the United States are familiar with the Charles River Basin through either personal visits or seeing it on television. Coverage of such events as the Boston Marathon or Celtic, Bruins, or Red Sox games often include shots of the skyline, taken from Cambridge, with the Charles in the foreground.

The MDC parkland along the Charles is part of the Charles River Reservation, which has parcels of land from the Museum of Science in Boston to Cutler Park in Dedham. It's this park system that saves the Charles from becoming just another urban river, lined with factories and commercial development. Credit for this farsighted planning begins with Charles Eliot, who proposed the creation of a metropolitan park system in 1892. He recognized that action must be taken to save some natural areas along the river for everyone to use. Eliot's plea rings true today: "Here is a district possessed of a charming river already much resorted to for pleasure, the banks of which are continually in danger of spoilation at the hands of their private owners." From this idea, the Metropolitan District Commission, which supervises the Charles from Boston to the South Natick Dam, was born.

Until I visited other urban areas and saw the development that crowds right to the edge of their rivers, I didn't fully appreciate what we have here. The green patches of shoreline near Harvard University and Boston University are filled with students during warm weather. The settings for these institutions wouldn't be half as attractive without the Charles.

Beyond the Boston University Bridge, which lies at the edge of Back Bay and downtown Boston, is the lower Charles River Basin—a part of the river just about everyone is familiar with. When I walk along this well-known section of the Charles, I often find myself wondering whether Boston made the Charles, or the river made the city.

# The Lakes District to the Boston University Bridge

## PADDLING

*One Car:* Park at Recreation Park on Recreation Road. Put in here and paddle upstream under Route 128 to the pastoral setting of the Leo J. Martin Memorial Golf Course. The Charles passes through marshland, woods, and the golf course fairways. Good birding and fishing for largemouths, pickerel, panfish, and perhaps a northern pike.

*Two Cars:* Leave one car at the MDC launch off Woerd Avenue or at Forest Grove Park, also off Woerd Avenue, on the Newton-Waltham line. Then drive to either the Recreation Road launch site or the duck feeding station off Route 30 in Weston to launch. As you head downstream toward your car, you will pass through the many coves and setbacks of the Lakes District. Sometimes it's hard to find the true river channel through the many twists, turns, and coves, so it's best to have a topographical map. This is an exposed area, so avoid canoeing on windy days and bring the necessary supplies. Don't forget a large net if you are going after pike. About two and a half miles; no portages.

## RIVER WALKS

The Charles River Reservation is a string of MDC parklands that run along the river in various places. My favorite is the North Beacon Street–Charles River Road area, which abuts the river in Watertown.

Another great place for a stroll is Mount Feake Cemetery, with its towering oak, maple, beech, and spruce trees.

*A handsome couple enjoying a paddle on the Charles.*

Stroll along the cemetery's River Avenue and Quinobequin Avenue, which provide good views of the river and its ducks and birds. Jogging is not permitted during working hours.

And, of course, there is always the most famous river walk of all: the Esplanade in Boston.

## BIKING

The western end of the Paul Dudley White Bike Path begins at Galen Street, and it's possible to bike and skate along this path all the way into Boston and Cambridge. There are MDC parking lots along Soldiers Field Road and wide grassy banks for picnicking. You can make a nice loop of seven miles running from Galen Street to the Eliot Bridge on one side of the river and return on the opposite side. (If you want to add approximately five more miles you can continue on to the B.U. Bridge.)

You won't be traveling in solitude as you would be in Dover and Sherborn, but the action around the river—ranging from windsurfers to in-line skaters—makes a day of biking seem like a festive occasion. The greenway along the river has benches for resting and taking in such sites as sailboats, scullers, sunbathers, musicians, and vendors peddling their goods.

## BIRDING

The entire Lakes District, from Recreation Park to the Moody Street dam, offers good birding because of the many coves and wetland areas. Most of the wading birds and waterfowl mentioned in earlier chapters can be seen here, as well as an occasional surprise visitor such as an osprey stopping here during the fall migration. Because this area does have its fair share of small powerboats, birding is best just after dawn or on weekdays in the spring and fall. Even downstream from the Moody Street dam along Soldiers Field Road, birding can be productive, with mergansers, night herons, and ruddy ducks seen. Mount Auburn Cemetery is an especially good birding spot during spring and fall migration, and it's a wonderful place for a stroll, particularly in May when many of the trees, bushes, and flowers are in bloom.

## ANGLING

Largemouth bass and carp all over the river, bullheads on the slow water, pickerel in the setbacks, and northern pike in the Lakes District.

## PICNICKING

Forest Grove Park in Waltham and MDC parkland from Galen Street east to the basin and Esplanade.

## POINTS OF HISTORIC INTEREST

- Walk the grounds of Brook Farm on Baker Street in West Roxbury.
- Norumbega Tower (erected by Eban Horsford in 1889 to honor his theory that the Vikings had been here) is located on Norumbega Road near the Weston-Waltham line.

## CANOE AND KAYAK RENTAL

Concessions along Soldiers Field Road often rent canoes on weekends. Members of a public sailing group can rent sailboats and windsurfers from Community Boating, (617) 523-1038, at 21 Embankment Road, Boston, MA 02114.

Charles River Canoe & Kayak Service
2401 Commonwealth Ave., Newton
617-965-5110

# 8

## The City River

TECHNICALLY, THE CHARLES River Basin starts at the Watertown Dam, which would make it about nine miles long. However, when I think of the basin, I don't include the portions flowing through Watertown, Brighton, Allston, or the western portions of Cambridge. To my way of thinking, the real basin starts at the Boston University Bridge, where the river begins to widen considerably, giving it the appearance of a long and narrow lake.

Although canoeing is permitted, the hazards are many: powerboats, sailboats, scullers, crews, and high winds all can harass a small canoe. Leave the basin to them.

This city river bears little resemblance to the upper Charles; joggers and roller skaters take the place of muskrat and herons, while organized events like the Head of the Charles Regatta replace solitary canoe outings. Held each year on the next-to-last Sunday in October, the regatta is the world's largest single-day rowing event. Boats from all over the country, and even outside the United States, compete on the Charles. Throngs of people line the three-mile

*Back Bay seen through the masts of sailboats on the Charles.*

156 • • • *Exploring the Hidden Charles*

route, enjoying the festivities. I've watched the event a couple of times, and, while it certainly is fun, I prefer to spend free Sundays on the *other* Charles, the upstream section that sees more ducks than boaters. And that's the beauty of this river—it can accommodate a loner like myself or host social events like the regatta.

I prefer to enjoy the city river with as few interruptions as possible, and that means biking on a Sunday morning. It's amazing what ghost towns Watertown, Cambridge, and Boston become at that time. Whipping down deserted city streets can be exhilarating, and the paths along the Esplanade afford panoramic views of the river that somehow look crisper and cleaner when no other people are about.

But clean and crisp are hardly adjectives I'd use for the water quality of the lower Charles. Sail-boarders may fall in from time to time without any ill effects, but I wouldn't make a habit of it. The primary pollution culprit is the outdated sewage system that overflows whenever there is a heavy rainstorm. It is estimated that twenty outlets overflow up to twenty-eight times a year. Nevertheless, considering the river's past, it has come a long way. In a past issue of *Yankee* magazine, Linda Morganroth describes the Back Bay area of the Charles in the early 1800s: "From time to time a dead horse would wash up, along with formerly attached human limbs and other miscellaneous anatomical parts that had floated down the Charles River from nearby Massachusetts General Hospital."

At the time, Back Bay as we know it didn't even exist; the area was a large tidal flat. The Charles River estuary and river mouth covered a significant section of Boston. Beginning in the early part of the nineteenth century, ambitious city leaders decided to drain the marsh and fill the wetlands.

Captain John Smith's reference to the Charles indicates that he was fooled by the tidal flats at the river's mouth: "The River cloth pearce many daies journies the intralls of that Countrie." Obviously, he didn't bother actually to go up the Charles. Before Prince Charles renamed the river, Captain Smith called it the Massachusetts River.

Captain Smith thought Massachusetts would be the perfect place for the English to settle: "...and then the Countrie of Massachusetts, which is the Paradise of all those parts. The Sea Coast as you passe, shews you all along large come fields and great troupes of well proportioned people...." He went on to extol the region's timber resources, fertile ground, ocean fisheries, and favorable climate.

Although most historians give Captain Smith the credit for discovering the Charles, Samuel de Champlain had actually explored the coast at an earlier date (and many historians would argue that the first Europeans to reach New England were Leif Ericson and his Vikings). Champlain kept an extensive journal of his 1605 trip to Massachusetts. He found the coast densely populated with Indians: "All along the shore there is a great deal of land cleared up and planted with Indian corn." Champlain describes one encounter with the Indians as follows: "...there came to us fifteen or sixteen canoes of savages. In some of them there were fifteen or sixteen who began to manifest great signs of joy, and made various harangues which we could not in the least understand." It was thought that Champlain elected not to explore the area on foot because there were simply too many Indians of unknown disposition.

Another entry in Champlain's journal is of significant interest to canoeists: the description of the incredible amount of work it took the Indians to make a dugout canoe. First, a large tree had to be cut with stone axes, then the vessel was shaped, and finally the inside was furrowed using a combination of slow-burning fire and scraping with sharpened stone.

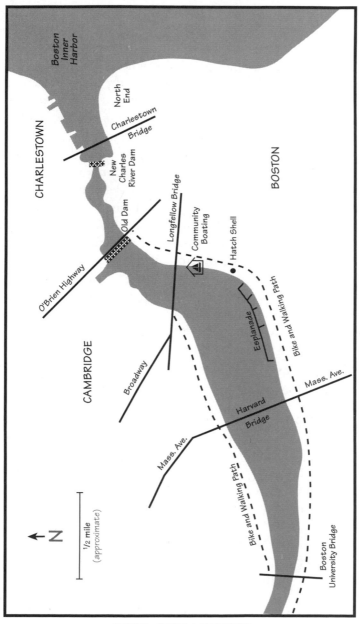

# THE CITY RIVER

While Champlain and Captain Smith recorded seeing numerous Indians along the coastline of Massachusetts, the Puritans encountered very few. In a two-year period, from 1615 to 1617, a plague broke out among the Indians and reduced their numbers by the thousands. This plague was probably a disease introduced by the Europeans, perhaps measles or bubonic plague, to which the Indians had no immunity. So, by 1630, when the Puritans started arriving in heavy numbers, they found the land around the mouth of the Charles almost completely devoid of natives. In fact, about the only person living on the Shawmut Peninsula, which we now call Boston, was William Blackstone, a British clergyman. Blackstone had settled along the south coast of the state at first but wished to escape the increasing number of people who were settling near Plymouth. In Boston, he found what he was looking for: a chance to live with nature in solitude. He was something of an early-day Thoreau. In fact, Blackstone's life reminds me of Thoreau's days at Walden, where he wrote, "Be a Columbus to whole new worlds within you, explore the Ocean of one's being alone." Imagine living as Blackstone did, having all of Boston as your own.

In the 1620s, Blackstone built his home beside a spring high atop what is now known as Beacon Hill. It must have been a beautiful place, with views of water in every direction. Unfortunately the peninsula where this hermit lived was the very place John Winthrop and his Puritan followers had their eyes on. Winthrop's Puritans had first settled in Charlestown, on the other side of the river, in the spring of 1630, but it wasn't long before they crossed the Charles, crowding Blackstone out of his paradise. Blackstone simply sold his land, packed his bags, and moved upstream, eventually going beyond the Charles all the way to a different river that now bears his name, the Blackstone.

The Puritans and other colonists set to work developing the peninsula they renamed Boston. At the time,

Boston's only connection to the mainland was a thin strip of land called "the neck," located close to where Washington Street now lies. Travel to the mainland either had to pass over the neck or be by boat. In 1662, the Great Bridge was built, a rickety wooden structure spanning the Charles between Brighton and Cambridge—one still had to cross the neck before reaching the bridge. Bostonians dreamed of a more solid bridge that could span the much wider stretch of river closer to the heart of the growing settlement. But they would wait more than a hundred years; in fact, a revolution would be fought before a bridge was built in Boston.

The Charles played a part in much of New England's history, and the American Revolution was no exception. The year 1775 found the colonists hiding arms in Concord, Massachusetts, to be used against the British. British soldiers, commanded by General Gage, were based in Boston, and they formulated a secret plan to raid Concord and capture the weapons. The patriots uncovered the plan, however, and they watched the British for any signs of a move. The British couldn't just slip out of Boston; they had to cross the neck or the Charles, so watching them was easy.

On April 18, patriot spies saw the redcoats gathering at night along the banks of the Charles. Paul Revere, who had already rowed across the river, set out to spread the alarm (as did William Dawes by way of Boston Neck). Historian Richard Brown, in *Massachusetts: A Bicentennial History,* records: "The British raiding party got off to a late start and then delayed its march from Charlestown." Did crossing the Charles prove more difficult than anticipated? If the British had arrived in Lexington during the night's darkness, rather than at dawn, would shots have been fired?

Just two months after the Battles of Lexington and Concord, the Charles once again was a factor in the Revolution. June 1775 found the British still hunkered down in

*Longfellow Bridge is in the foreground, Beacon Hill in the background. Longfellow Bridge has the best "city view" of the river.*

Boston, surrounded by thousands of armed patriots. General Gage was still commanding the British army, and he knew the patriots could use cannon against him from either Dorchester Heights or the hills of Charlestown. Writing to England, he bemoaned the fact that "our supplies from the country are cut off." Gage began making preparations to take the two hills of Charlestown: Breed's Hill and Bunker Hill. Once again, the patriots learned of his plans, and on the night of June 16, 1775, they moved their own troops onto Breed's Hill, leaving reinforcements on Bunker Hill.

When dawn broke the next morning Gage realized what had happened, and preparations were immediately made to storm the hill before the patriots could become entrenched. But first the redcoats would have to cross the Charles. No fewer than 2,200 British troops had to be ferried across the river—a crossing that did not take place until noon, allowing the patriots more time to dig in.

The ragtag patriot militiamen must have had their doubts as they looked down on the Charles and saw the scarlet-clad British, bayonets gleaming, rowing across the river. But the patriots fought well, inflicting a great many casualties before they ran low on powder and were forced to give up the hill. This battle gave the Americans the confidence they needed; they now knew they could hold their own against the exalted British army. (The battle also spawned two famous sayings. Colonel John Stark, who commanded a group of patriots from New Hampshire, is said to have urged his men to join the battle by crying, "Live free or die!" And Colonel William Prescott, the leader of all the Americans at Breed's and Bunker Hills, instructed his troops, "Don't fire until you see the white of their eyes.")

At the end of the Revolutionary War, the citizens of Massachusetts turned their attention back to the building of Boston. A group of investors, led by John Hancock, proposed to build a bridge over the Charles, connecting Boston to Charlestown. Although many were skeptical that a bridge of this size could be built, the investors' gamble paid off handsomely when they began receiving the tolls from the bridge, completed in 1786. Supported by seventy-five piers of oak timber, the bridge was 1,503 feet long—the Charles had finally been crossed and no longer did Boston have the feel of an island.

Bostonians next focused their engineering energies on the Back Bay, an area of vast mud flats and saltwater marshes. As early as 1799, small coves and scattered wetlands were being filled in around the city, using earth taken off the tops of Boston's hills. In 1857, the filling of Back Bay began in earnest. Boston's hills had been just about leveled, and gravel had to be brought in by railroad all the way from Needham. Over the next several years, the boundaries of the Charles were reshaped, groomed, molded, corralled, and tamed. No matter how you look at it, the last miles of the Charles have been formed more by man than by nature.

The ramifications of the filling in of Back Bay still remain with us. Trinity Church is a good example of an older building's sensitivity to fluctuations in the water table beneath Back Bay. The church was built in 1877, and the construction of choice during those years was to support the structure by sinking a great number of wooden pilings. Forty-five hundred spruce pilings stand beneath the church. The pilings, each about one foot in diameter, have been driven down through the fill and muck into the Boston blue clay, which is well above bedrock. These wooden pilings work just fine, so long as they stay wet—the water, in a sense, keeps them petrified. Trouble, in the form of rot, begins when the pilings go dry, or when they alternate between being wet and dry. Bacteria sets in, followed by rot, which could cause the entire building to collapse.

*A view of the Esplanade and the Hatch Shell.*

Keeping water around the pilings is not as easy as it sounds. The water level is sensitive to any major construction in the area, such as sewer, subway, or building erection. Over the years, there have been various incidents of fluctuating water levels causing structural damage to older buildings. In the late 1920s, the front landing area of the Boston Public Library suffered extensive damage, and even today the homes along Brimmer Street, near Beacon Hill, have incurred damage costing millions of dollars to repair.

To get a better idea of the headaches caused by reshaping Boston and the Charles in the 1800s, I met with Richard Merrill, building manager of Trinity Church. Before he gave me a tour, he showed me how he must check the water levels beneath the building on a weekly basis. He does this by inserting an electronic device into long pipes that have been driven deep into the ground at scattered intervals around the church. In addition, there is a backup alarm system that would sound if the water drops to a dangerous level. The water level is not equal on all sides of the church; for example, on the John Hancock side it is lower than on the Boylston Street side. Even more surprising is that the entire Back Bay area has sunk nine inches in the last hundred years, as the fill settles and becomes compacted.

Merrill showed me the ancient cellar of Trinity and told me how the water was monitored at the turn of the century. It seems that there was always water in the church cellar at that time. A small rowboat was kept there, and if anyone noticed the rowboat listing, that meant the water level had dropped and the base of the boat was resting on the ground!

We walked over to a manhole in one corner of the cellar. It was installed in the early 1930s to allow a visual check of water levels and to provide access to the pilings. After we removed the old wooden cover, water could be seen about five feet beneath the floor.

Next, we walked toward the portion of the cellar beneath the front of the church. I could clearly see the four great granite piers upon which the church tower rests. It is under these pyramid-shaped supports that the bulk of the wooden piles stand. The tower weighs twelve million pounds—quite a load for wooden pilings stuck in clay.

Before we reached the narrow staircase that would take us back upstairs, I noticed a set of ropes attached to pulleys. "That," said Merrill, "is the old coffin lift, the only one remaining in the country. The church sexton used to act as the undertaker, and this room was the mortuary." It was clear that the lift hadn't been used in some time, but what an aid it must have been—coffins could be raised and lowered quite easily on the lift, rather than carried up and down the stairs.

Merrill gave me a copy of an engineering report, written by Robert Treat Paine in 1935, that reviews problems faced in the Back Bay during the early 1900s as a result of fluctuations in the underground water levels. It reads like a mystery novel.

In the 1920s the walls of the Boston Public library showed cracks, and investigations showed that the wooden piles beneath the front of the library had rotted due to lowered underground water levels. Why had the water dropped? A Committee on Foundations was formed, and several possible causes were reviewed. Did subway or new sewer construction affect the water level? Could an enormous sump pump, like the one in the Copley Square Hotel, have sucked the Back Bay dry? Even the possibility of an earthquake and its effects on underground water tables was explored. Maps were drawn of old coves and creek beds for engineers to examine. Some thought the solution to the problem might be to pipe water from the Charles River Basin to Copley Square.

The committee and a host of engineers were stumped. The public became aware of the mystery when the *Boston*

*Herald* printed an article on January 1, 1933, entitled "Back Bay Area Going Dry—Engineers Mystified."

Finally, a number of test wells were sunk in various spots around the Back Bay. These led engineers to suspect that a new sewer pipe beneath St. James Avenue was carrying away too much water. The mayor then appointed another committee, the Technology Committee, to ascertain what should be done about the problem. There was a real fear that the church or library would someday collapse, killing scores of people. The solution was reached when the offending sewer was sealed to stop the excess diversion of water. And so the "drying" of the Back Bay was halted.

In 1884 the Back Bay was almost completely filled; yet there were still complaints about the exposed mud flats along the river. Downstream from the Watertown Dam, the Charles was still a tidal estuary that rose and fell, creating unpleasant odors. The state Board of Health and the Metropolitan Parks Commission reported that "the banks of the river and the exposed mud flats have become from year to year more offensive...." The only way to keep the river from rising and falling was to create a dam. And so the next great assault on the Charles began in the early 1900s, with the construction of the Charles River Dam.

The dam, completed in 1910, was built at the site of the old Craige Bridge (where the Museum of Science now stands). By stopping the flow of salt water into the Charles, the dam in effect turned a salt water estuary into a freshwater pond. The tides no longer affected the river and a stable water level was maintained, allowing the mud flats to be filled and landscaped into what is now the Esplanade, which was greatly expanded in 1931.

The Charles River Dam was a success to the extent that it kept the basin stable; however, some salt water continued to filter in. Even more troublesome was the fact that the dam could not release flood waters from the basin during high tide. High tides meant that the water outside the dam was higher than the water on the basin side, and the gravity-driven flow of water exiting the basin was halted. During heavy spring runoffs, rainstorms, or hurricanes, the water backed up inside the Charles River basin, causing severe flooding. A new dam with pumps to carry flood water out of the basin during high tide was needed.

The site selected for the new Charles River Dam was about a half-mile to the east of the old dam, toward Boston's Inner Harbor (where the former Warren Avenue linked Boston to Charlestown). Construction of the dam was completed in 1981.

I recently toured the dam and saw the six massive pumps, each capable of pumping 630,000 gallons of water a minute into the harbor. But what really caught my eye was the fishway located just outside the enclosed pumping house. During heavy spring spawning runs, it's possible to see shad and herring heading through the fishway or resting in one of the twenty-nine connecting pools. Unfortunately, the fishway has not been a total success because during high tide the current flowing through the fishway and out of the basin comes to a stop, and when the current stops, so do the fish. Anadromous fish instinctively swim against the flow to spawn upstream; without a current they do not recognize the fishway as marking the beginning of their freshwater river journey.

The area around the New Charles River Dam is worth a visit. Besides the dam itself, the MDC operates the Charles River Information Center at the Charlestown end of the dam, with a number of interesting river photos and an observation window overlooking the dam's three locks. My favorite part of the information center is the audiovisual show, which gives a brief historical overview of the river as well as information on the dams and water levels.

The view upstream from the dam is one of highways and commercial buildings; however, the harbor view from the Charlestown Bridge shows the waters of the Charles

*Enjoying a sail.*

mingling with those of the bay, and in the distance, the masts of the USS *Constitution,* "Old Ironsides." The ship is berthed at the approximate spot where Paul Revere landed when he crossed the Charles in advance of the redcoats. Beyond Old Ironsides rises the Bunker Hill Monument.

It's a shame we cannot see the land as Champlain and Captain Smith first saw it, nor will we ever see the lower Charles as it was in its natural state. But at least folks can

*At the end of the river, a view across Boston inner harbor at the Bunker Hill Monument and Old Ironsides.*

take full advantage of the recreational opportunities offered by the man-made Charles. In fact, the basin has become *too* popular on many summer weekends. Among the craft vying for water space are the many powerboats moored in the river's various yacht clubs and the scullers from colleges and private clubs. MDC police try their best to keep the area safe, but the overcrowding causes its share of accidents nevertheless. The best time to be on the river is in the early morning, like the handful of "bassers" who have found surprisingly good largemouth bass fishing right in the shadow of the city.

Perhaps it's the area's college students who really "own" the basin, and with so many universities along the Charles, it surely must be the "smartest" river in the world. It's the student pranks that catch my eye, such as the MIT students who laid a fraternity brother end-over-end to measure the Massachusetts Avenue bridge. The brother's name was Smoot, and he must have been a fairly small guy, because the bridge is 364.4 Smoots and 1 ear long. (Now when I drive over any Charles River bridge, I mumble something like "about 40 Smoots long.")

My favorite bridge is the one with the best "city view" of the river—the Longfellow Bridge. I love this bridge; it was designed for people as well as for cars and subways. Its four ornate turrets, with landings around each column, are perfect spots for river-gazing. The bridge was named after Henry Wadsworth Longfellow, who for forty-five years wrote from his home near the banks of the Charles in Cambridge. Before the existing bridge was built, Longfellow would often visit the original West Boston Bridge, the view from which he described in his poem "The Bridge": "I stood on the bridge at midnight..."

The Charles has given inspiration to poets, philosophers, and presidents, but Longfellow acknowledged it best in 1841 when he wrote "To the River Charles":

*Low tide at the Cambridge embankment and flats as seen from West Boston Bridge, July 11, 1902, 10:00 A.M.*

River! that in silence windest
Through the meadows bright and free,
Till at length thy rest thou findest
 In the bosom of the sea!

Thou hast taught me, Silent River!
Many a lesson, deep and long;
Thou hast been a generous giver;
I can give thee but a song.

Where yon shadowy woodlands hide thee,
And thy waters disappear,
Friends I love have dwelt beside thee,
And have made thy margin dear.

Longfellow knew this was a special river. Man may have shaped the Charles, but the Charles helped shape the nation. The river has witnessed the evolution of America: Indians, the coming of the Europeans, and the Revolution as a nation was born. Later, the river came under attack from dams, pollution, and unchecked development along its banks. Much of the river has been either ignored or mistreated, and only in the past few years has there been a modest rekindling of appreciation and interest in the Charles. Most of the focus seems to be on the city river, but let's not forget the upper Charles, which is so vulnerable to exploitation. Let us guard it wisely.

# The City River

## RIVER WALKS

There are numerous sidewalks all along the City River on either side, including the most famous river walk—the Esplanade.

## BIKING

The Esplanade area is famous for its paved walking/ biking/in-line skating paths along the Charles. It's possible to make a loop of the Charles almost entirely on paved paths closed to motorized vehicles running from the B.U. Bridge to the Longfellow Bridge on the Boston side of the Charles and returning on the Cambridge side. This route is part of the Paul Dudley White Bike Path (it runs from Watertown to Boston and Cambridge, covering eighteen miles). Be warned that riding here does not offer the elbow room of the bike rides described earlier, and on sunny weekends the banks of the Charles are lined with folks looking for fresh air and exercise. (On Sundays in the spring, summer, and fall cars are prohibited from a 1.2-mile section of Memorial Drive, which allows for more skating and biking room.)

## BIRDING

In the basin you begin to see birds usually associated with the ocean, such as cormorants and gulls, but there are great blue herons and night herons as well. Because of the crowds on the Esplanade and all the different boaters on the river, viewing is best in the early morning.

## ANGLING

There is surprisingly good angling in the basin for large-mouth bass.

## PICNICKING

Between Waltham and Boston are numerous walking/biking trails and all along the way are picnic tables on both sides of the river.

## POINTS OF HISTORIC INTEREST

- Visit the Charles River Museum of Industry, located along the banks of the Charles in an old mill complex, to see displays of automobiles, textile manufacturing, and clock making (call 617-893-5410).
- Visit Trinity Church in the Copley Square section of the Back Bay.
- Walk the Longfellow Bridge and enjoy views of the river and Beacon Hill from its ornate turrets.
- Visit the Charles River Information Center at the Charlestown end of the New Charles River Dam.
- Visit Old Ironsides and Bunker Hill Monument in Charlestown.

## CANOE AND KAYAK RENTAL

Concessions along Soldiers Field Road often rent canoes on weekends. Members of a public sailing group can rent sailboats and windsurfers from Community Boating (617-523-1038) at 21 Embankment Road, Boston, MA 02114.

# Epilogue

THERE IS A THREE-MILE stretch of the Charles, located about fifty-five river miles from the bay, that I've visited well over a hundred times—yet I still don't really know it. More than once I've taken a friend here for a river tour, only to have the Charles throw a curve at the tour guide. I remember telling Cogs, "Nobody ever comes here"— only to have a fleet of canoes go by ten minutes later. On that same trip, we reached some quick water at a bridge, and I said, "The left channel is the one to take." We did, and scraped and battered the canoe, coming within a whisker of capsizing. The surprises keep coming and I keep going back. About the only sure bet is that my excursions always run later than planned. It's easy to lose track of time on the water, and my wife, Mary Ellen, only laughs when I say I'll be home at such-and-such a time. I always go around one more bend or fish one more pool—curiosity is a powerful force.

On my first day paddling the river in 1997, I put in at Central Street in Needham and went upstream into the coves. As I pulled away from the launch site, the traffic noise was replaced by bird sounds: two hawks screeched as they circled overhead; geese honked loudly, as small groups seemed to be flying every which way; and red-winged black-birds, stationed in the reeds, sang their squeaky "kong-ka-ree." The water was high, and in the main channel it took a bit of work to make headway against the current. Unlike just a few miles upstream, where the Charles penetrates through a shadowy tangle of trees, this stretch is wide open, and even an April sun can get quite warm. I peeled off my coat, then shirt, and by noontime, I had the beginnings of a sunburn.

The area is wide enough to handle low-horsepower outboard motors, and I saw a little bass boat tucked in the far end of a cove where the water warms faster than the main channel, which usually means better spring fishing. The basser and I exchanged greetings, and he said, "I could stay out here all day long, it's so peaceful." I knew what he meant, and I responded that I felt like "paddling right through the night." He looked at me like I was daft, but that's how I felt—it was exhilarating to be back on the river after months of winter hibernation.

As I continued working my way upstream, I let my mind wander and my arms fell into rhythmic paddling. I really didn't have a particular destination in mind, nor did I have any worldly problems to sort out. Thoughts flowed unencumbered just like the slow, brown water beneath me. As I rounded a bend, my daydreaming was halted by another sighting of a great blue heron hiding motionless in the reeds. Instead of flying off, the bird just watched me silently, and I was careful not to make any sudden movements or turn the canoe toward it. Perhaps the heron thought I didn't see it, but its gray coloring among the golds and browns of dried vegetation made it easy to spot. I slowly raised my camera, and after fifteen years of trying to capture one of these elusive creatures on film, I *finally* got the shot I wanted.

The next day my brother, Mark, and I had intended to return to this spot, but the fickle April weather had turned too cold for canoeing. We settled for a walk beside the

Charles. As we strolled down a riverbank trail, an object stuck in the mud beneath a big oak tree caught Mark's attention. The object turned out to be the top half of a colonial clay pipe, common in the eighteenth and nineteenth centuries.

The pipe reminded me that others, from a time long past, knew the river as I do. This riverbank trail is something of a secret now, but how many people over countless generations have walked along the Charles? And what did the river look like to them?

The base of the giant oak tree would be a fine place to sit, smoke a pipe, and watch the river go by. Someday soon I must come back here—no paddling, no fishing rod, no camera—just the river and me, like the owner of the colonial pipe.

Norman Maclean, author of *A River Runs through It*, says, "Eventually, all things merge into one, and a river runs through it." The Charles has run through my life, and I've come to think of it as a friend. Perhaps I feel such affection for the river because it's occasionally abused and so often overlooked. Many people live along its banks, but few have bothered to give it more than a passing glance. It remains largely a hidden river waiting to be rediscovered.

The Charles surprised me with its subtle, peaceful character, and I learned its secrets only through repeated visits. What I've missed, I hope to capture in the future. I'm fond of saying that I feel like I own "my" stretch of the Charles and must do what I can to protect it. But the truth of the matter is, the river owns me.

# *About the Author*

I N HIS FREE TIME Michael Tougias enjoys hiking with his family, fishing, canoeing, and reading. When not writing or exploring, he volunteers his time to conservation efforts. He lives with his family in Franklin, Massachusetts.

Tougias is the author of several books about New England:

- *New England Wild Places*

- *Autumn Trails*

- *Quiet Places of Massachusetts*

- *Nature Walks in Eastern Massachusetts*

- *Nature Walks in Central Massachusetts*

- *Country Roads of Massachusetts*

- *Until I Have No Country* (A Novel of King Philip's Indian War)

- *A Taunton River Journey*

- *Cape Cod According to Thoreau and Beston*

Tougias gives narrated slide presentations for each of his books, including King Philip's Indian War. If you are interested in his slide presentations or his publications, please write to him at PO Box 72, Norfolk, MA 02056.

# About
# the AMC

Since 1876, the Appalachian Mountain Club has promoted the protection, enjoyment, and wise use of the mountains, rivers, and trails of the Northeast. The AMC believes that successful, long-term conservation depends on first-hand experience and enjoyment of the outdoors. A nonprofit organization, AMC's membership of more than 73,000 enjoy hiking, canoeing, skiing, walking, rock climbing, bicycling, camping, kayaking, and backpacking, while—at the same time—help to safeguard the environment. All AMC programs and facilities are open to the public.

## AMC Huts & Lodges

AMC offers unique overnight lodgings throughout the Northeast. Spend an overnight at one of eight huts, each a day's hike apart, in the White Mountains of New Hampshire, or drive to Bascom Lodge atop Mt. Greylock in western Massachusetts. Also accessible by car are Pinkham Notch Lodge or Crawford Hostel in New Hampshire, and Mohican Outdoor Center in the Delaware Water Gap of western New Jersey. For reservations, call 603-466-2727.

*Madison Spring Hut, one of the eight trailside huts maintained by the AMC, offers hikers hot meals, warm bunks, and mountain hospitality. (Paul Mozell)*

## AMC Outdoor Adventures

Whether you're new to the outdoors or an old hand, the AMC offers workshops and guided trips that will teach you new skills, refine your expertise, or just get you outside in good company. Choose from more than 100 workshops and adventures offered in New Hampshire, Massachusetts, New York, and New Jersey. Whether you're going solo, with your family and kids, or with friends, there is something for everyone.

Each of our 11 chapters—from Maine to Washington, D.C.—offers hundreds of activities close to home. Chapter leaders arrange hiking and bicycling trips and teach the basics of cross-country skiing, whitewater and flatwater canoeing, and other outdoor skills.

## Volunteering

If you like to hike, discover the lasting satisfaction that comes with volunteering to maintain or build trails. No

*Discover the outdoors with AMC! Sign up for a workshop to learn outdoor activity skills and enjoy the company of new friends. (Rob Burbank)*

experience is necessary—we'll teach you what you need to know. The AMC leads volunteer trail building and maintenance crews throughout the Northeast. Our professional and volunteer crews take great pride in maintaining 1,400 miles of trails throughout the region.

Paddlers can help clean up a river, monitor water quality, or help negotiate access with private landowners. Volunteering is a great way to give something back to the rivers and trails that have taken you to so many wonderful places.

## Conservation Leadership

Much of the northeast's outdoor recreation opportunities would not be possible without a commitment to protecting land and keeping trails, rivers, and mountains accessible. Since its founding, the AMC has been at the forefront of the conservation movement. AMC members fought for the creation of the White Mountain National Forest in 1911. More recently we have been active in protecting the Appalachian Trail corridor, improving access to and the health of rivers and land around hydroelectric dams, and improving water and air quality. Our conservation policies are backed by solid scientific research, conducted by our own professional researchers in conjunction with organizations such as the Harvard School of Public Health, Dartmouth College, U.S. Forest Service, and the National Park Service. We're working to keep our air clean and healthy, our waterfalls clear, our rivers running free, and recreational activities open.

## AMC Books & Maps

The AMC publishes an extensive line of books, including nature guides, New England history, outdoor skills, conservation, and our famous trail guides and maps. AMC guidebooks are essential companions for all kinds of outdoor adventures throughout the eastern U.S. Our publications are available at most bookstores and outdoor retailers as well as our main office in Boston and Pinkham Notch Visitor Center in New Hampshire. To order by phone, call 800-262-4455. Also available through the AMC is APPALACHIA, the country's oldest mountaineering and conservation journal.

## AMC Membership

We invite you to join the Appalachian Mountain Club and share the benefits of membership. Your membership includes a one-year subscription to *AMC Outdoors*, the Northeast's premier outdoor magazine—telling you where to go for outdoor recreation and keeping you informed on conservation issues. Members also enjoy discounts on AMC books, maps, workshops, and lodgings, as well as free affiliation to one of AMC's eleven chapters.

For more information on AMC, call 617-523-0636 or visit our website at www.outdoors.org. To join, send a check for $40 for an adult, or $65 for a family to AMC Membership, 5 Joy Street, Boston, MA 02108; or pay by Visa or MasterCard by calling 617-523-0636 .

# Bibliography

Alden, John R. "Revolutionary War in America." In *World Book Encyclopedia*. Chicago: Field Enterprises Educational Corp., 1963.

*AMC River Guide: Massachusetts, Connecticut, Rhode Island*. Boston: Appalachian Mountain Club Books, 1985.

Bickford, Walter, and Ute Janik Dymon, eds. *An atlas of Massachusetts River Systems*. Amherst: University of Massachusetts Press, 1990.

Brown, Richard D. *Massachusetts: A Bicentennial History*. New York: W. W. Norton, 1978.

Canby, Thomas Y. "The Search for the First Americans." *National Geographic*, September 1979.

Charles River Watershed Association. *Charles River Canoe Guide*. Auburndale, Mass.: Charles River Watershed Association, 1977.

Charles River Watershed Association and Thelma Fleishman. *Charles River Dams*. Auburndale, Mass.: Charles River Watershed Association, 1978.

Crawford, Michael J. *A History of Natick, Massachusetts.* Natick: Natick Historical Commission, 1978.

Dincauze, Dena F. "An Introduction to Archeology in the Greater Boston Area." *Archaeology of Eastern North America* Volume 2 (Spring 1974): pp. 39–67. Attleboro, Mass.: Eastern States Archeological Federation, 1974.

Dumanoski, Dianne. "For the State's Ospreys, These Are the Good Old Days." *Boston Globe,* February 5, 1990.

Gaines, Judith. "Of Hacks and Smoot." *Boston Globe,* April 1, 1991.

Hall, Max. *The Charles: The People's River.* Boston: David R. Godine, 1986.

Harris, John. "The Battle of Bunker Hill." *Boston Globe,* June 8, 1975.

Harris, John. *Boston Globe Historic Walks in Cambridge.* Chester, Conn.: Globe Pequot Press, 1986.

Howe, Henry F. *Prologue to New England.* New York: Farrar and Rinehart, 1943.

Howe, Henry F. *Salt Water Rivers of the Massachusetts Shore.* New York: Rinehart and Company, 1951.

Kay, Jane Holz. *Lost Boston.* Boston: Houghton Mifflin Co., 1980.

Longfellow, Henry Wadsworth. "To the River Charles." *The Complete Poetical Works of Henry Wadsworth Longfellow,* Cambridge Edition. Cambridge, Mass.: Houghton Mifflin Co., Riverside Press, 1863.

Lyons, Janet, and Sandra Jordan. *Walking the Wetlands.* New York: John Wiley and Sons, 1989.

Macowan, Florence Lovell. "History of Natick" (manuscript), 1938–1941. Morse Institute Library. Natick, Mass.

Maclean, Norman. *A River Runs through It.* Chicago: University of Chicago Press, 1976.

Madson, John. *Up on the River: An Upper Mississippi Chronicle.* New York: Nick Lyons Books, 1985.

Massachusetts Audubon Society. *Broadmoor Wildlife Sanctuary.* South Natick, Mass.: Massachusetts Audubon Society.

Mavrides, Melanie. "Landfill critics vow to continue legal skirmish against MWRA." *Boston Sunday Globe.* December 23, 1990.

Metcalf, Leonard. "The Echo Lake Dam, at Milford, Ma." Engineering paper, Boston, 1903.

Metropolitan District Commission. *Welcome to the New Charles River Dam.* Boston: Metropolitan District Commission.

Metropolitan District Commission, Susan Griffin, and Leanne DelVecchio. *MDC Reservations and Facilities Guide.* Boston: Metropolitan District Commission Public Information Office.

Morganroth, Linda. *The Back Bay of Boston.* Dublin, N.H.: *Yankee,* December 1990.

Noanet Garden Club and The Trustees of Reservations. *Noanet Woodlands Reservation*. Beverly, Mass.: The Trustees of Reservations.

Nowak, Edward. "A Sleeping Giant: The Charles River." *The Fisherman*, August 1988.

Paine, Robert Treat. *Trinity Church in the City of Boston*. (The Church Endangered by the Low Level of the Ground Water. How the Danger has been Temporarily Averted.), April 1935.

Perry, John, and Jane G. Perry. *The Sierra Club Guide to the Natural Areas of New England*. San Francisco: Sierra Club Books, 1990.

Phillips, John C., and Thomas D. Cabot. *Quick-Water and Smooth: A Canoeist's Guide to New England Rivers*. Brattleboro, Vt.: Stephen Daye Press, 1935.

Pollock, Robert. *Out to Norumbega* (pamphlet).

Powers, John. "Unbuilt Boston." *Boston Globe Magazine*, December 30, 1990.

Russell, Howard S. *Indian New England Before the Mayflower*. Hanover, N.H.: University Press of New England, 1980.

Scheller, William G. *More Country Walks near Boston*. Boston: Appalachian Mountain Club Books, 1984.

Siegler, Hilbert R. *Yankee Wildlife*. Orford, N.H.: Equity Publishing, 1982.

Skerrett, P. J. "Purple Weeds Invade Wetlands." *Boston Sunday Globe,* August 19, 1990.

Stowe, Harriet Elizabeth Beecher. *Old Town Folks.* Edited by Henry F. May. Cambridge: Harvard University Press, Belknap Press, 1966.

"The Streamer." Auburndale, Mass. Charles River Watershed Association, November 1990.

Talabach, Michele. "Millis Roots Noted by Local Historian." *The Country Gazette.* Franklin, Mass. July 17, 1985.

Thompson, Leslie P. "The Carp." In *Fisherman's Bounty,* edited by Nick Lyons. New York: Simon and Schuster, 1988.

Thoreau, Henry David. *Walden and Other Writings.* Edited by Joseph Wood Krutch. New York: Bantam Books, 1962.

Tilden, William. *History of the Town of Medfield, Massachusetts 1650–1886.* Boston: George H. Ellis Publisher, 1887.

Tourtellot, Arthur B. *The Charles.* New York: Rinehart and Company, 1941.

The Trustees of Reservations. *A Guide to Properties of The Trustees of Reservations.* Beverly, Mass.: The Trustees of Reservations.

Vaughn, Alden T. *New England Frontier: Puritans and Indians 1620-1675.* Boston: Little, Brown, 1965.

Weber, Ken. *Canoeing Massachusetts, Rhode Island &* *Connecticut.* Somerset, NH: New Hampshire Publishing Co., 1980.

Whitehill, Walter Muir. *Boston: A Topographical History.* Cambridge: Harvard University Press, Belknap Press, 1959.

# Maps

# Recreation Guides